CHANGING THE LANDSCAPE:

ENDING VIOLENCE~ACHIEVING EQUALITY

EXECUTIVE SUMMARY/NATIONAL ACTION PLAN

CANADIAN PANEL ON

VIOLENCE AGAINST WOMEN

© Minister of Supply and Services Canada–1993

Catalogue No. SW45-1/1993E

ISBN # 0-660-15185-5
Also available in French
Printed in Canada

CANADIAN PANEL ON VIOLENCE AGAINST WOMEN

PANEL MEMBERS

Co-Chair
Pat Freeman Marshall

Co-Chair
Marthe Asselin Vaillancourt

Judy Hughes
Mobina Jaffer
Diane Lemieux
Eva McKay

Dr. Peter Jaffe
Ginette Larouche
Donna Lovelace

ABORIGINAL CIRCLE MEMBERS

Claudette Dumont-Smith
Winnifred Giesbrecht

Martha Flaherty
Jeanne McDonald

ADVISORY COMMITTEE MEMBERS

Sally Ballingall
Judge Douglas Campbell
Jurgen Dankwort
Edna Elias
Dr. Patricia Horsham
Jennifer Mercer
Dorothy Reso Hickman
Constable Jane Spaans
Esmeralda Thornhill

Hélène Cadrin
Colleen Croft-Cannuli
Dr. Michael Dixon
Ron Ghitter
Pearl McKenzie
Soeur Cécile Renault
Dr. Philip Smith
Christine Spénard-Godbout
Germaine Vaillancourt

Acknowledgement

The Panel benefitted from the expertise of the members of the Advisory Committee, each of whom possesses vast knowledge about violence, as researchers, lawyers or front-line workers. We thank the Advisory Committee members most sincerely for their contributions.

SECRETARIAT STAFF

Executive Director
Abby Hoffman
(June 1992 - July 1993)

Linda Blackwell
(August 1991 - March 1992)

Senior Advisor — Administration
Eloise Ryckman

Senior Adviser — Communications
Nicole Bourget

Senior Advisor — Liaison
Hélène Dwyer-Renaud

Senior Advisor — Research
Bonnie Diamond

Azaletch Asfaw
Jacqueline Barney
Michelle Bougie
Kirsten Cowen
Louise Delisle
Sandra Fox
Edith Garneau
Louise Gingras-Papineau
Nupur Gogia
Murielle Goneau
Mara Indri
Marcelle Lapointe
Lise Leach
Nicole Loreto
Guy Marcoux
Mary McBride
Marika Morris
Lise Nadeau
Karen O'Reilly
Line Poirier
Martine Rochon
Patricia Saulis
Margaret Shisko
Michelle Simms
Jennifer Tiller
Paula Walters

Linda Babulic
Roger Bélanger
Dave Cooper
Robert D'Aoust
Nathalie Ethier
Fay Frankland
Debbie Gibson
Carol Ann Godo
Denise Gomes
Jackie Holt
Lorraine Lapierre
Danielle Larose
Briar Long
Suzanne Madère
Elaine McArdle
Laura McFarlane
Gail Myles
Tracey O'Hearn
Josée Parisien
Tanya Rhodes
Marie Saikaley
Keith Sero
Laura Simmermon
Jo-Anne Stovel
Mary Trafford
Jeanne d'Arc Woods

Acknowledgement:

*In addition to the individuals listed above, the Panel would like
to thank the many people and organizations whose contributions
of time, energy and enthusiasm in various voluntary and professional
capacities were vital to the work of the Panel. In particular, a special
debt of gratitude is owed to the consultation agents, communication
agents, local organizers and interpreters who provided invaluable
support during the Panel's cross-Canada consultation process.*

CONTENTS

EXECUTIVE SUMMARY

THE NATIONAL ACTION PLAN

APPENDICES

CO-CHAIRS' MESSAGE

The Canadian Panel on Violence Against Women has just completed a unique and sometimes haunting journey. It was arduous, not because of its physical dimensions, but because of it psychological and political implications. Our report documents, more comprehensively than ever before, the unacceptable reality which many women in Canada have endured for decades but whose existence most Canadians have chosen to deny.

Canada's image abroad is that of a country with a high standard of living — a country dedicated to promoting peace in the world; a country where women have access to post-secondary education, and freedom of expression; a country where women are free to pursue the occupation they choose and to move about without constraint.

But the Panel learned that Canadian women are all too familiar with inequality and violence which tether them to lives few in the world would choose to lead. Canadian women have not enjoyed freedom of expression; rather, their fear makes them reluctant to speak out about the violence they experience. Canadian institutions have contributed to this situation — by denying that such violence can exist, they have supported misogyny and abuse of power.

Women came to the Panel with great generosity of spirit, hoping that by telling their truths and their stories, the lives of other women may be freed from violence. The breadth and depth of suffering described by them and now etched in our minds and in this report is our most profound impression of the Canadian landscape. By resolving to take action to eliminate violence against women, we can honour those women and change the landscape for future generations.

Many times the Panel members wished others in Canada could have been present to hear the truth, to see and understand the reality of the violence, and to confront the tolerance of violence. Our report will bring some of these experiences to you.

The Canadian experience was revealed to the Panel through face-to-face testimonies with thousands of individuals in 139 communities, in the 800 submissions we received and in our research. In tour after tour, at hearing upon hearing, in each of the provinces and the territories, women's voices told us of the horrors they endured. Through descriptions of the violence they survived, including the inadequate, ineffective and inappropriate responses to that violence they so often received, the link between inequality and vulnerability to violence was inextricably forged. It is abundantly and indisputably clear that women will not be free from violence until there is equality, and equality cannot be achieved until the violence and the threat of violence is eliminated from women's lives. This link is the foundation of our report. We know that the acknowledgement of this relationship has made our work and the task of implementing the report all the more challenging.

The tolerance of violence, in both principle and practice, has cost Canadian women dearly. One of the most tragic conclusions from our journey is the recognition that much of the violence women have endured was preventable. Solutions must be based on the fact that there is a high level of tolerance of violence, and therefore, that a policy of zero tolerance must be adopted by all levels of government – as well as within each and every organization in society.

We believe that a society that adopts zero tolerance of violence is a society that supports the basic human rights of each individual. It is a society which recognizes the importance of the United Nations *Universal Declaration of Human Rights* and the *Canadian Charter of Rights and Freedoms*, and the commitments they make to the right to security of the person, full entitlement to the protection and benefit of the law and, of course, the right to life.

While the Panel was doing its work, we were very aware there was a great deal happening in the world around us. But while commissions and inquests were helping to identify the problems and solutions, and while new laws were being created, women continued to suffer from violence. The tentative responses of the international community to the systematic rapes of women in Bosnia-Hercegovina were constant reminders to us that tolerance of violence against women knows no geographic boudaries.

Along with very different types of expertise and experience, the Panel and Aboriginal Circle members brought to their work a common vision of a better, safer society for all women and for everyone. Each member's commitment to that vision helped us through many difficult days. The activities of the Panel and the Aboriginal Circle were sustained and enhanced by the dedication of the secretariat staff members who worked tirelessly to ensure completion of the work. We have all worked in a way that we hope is faithful to the experiences of the women from whom we heard.

We wish to send a message of hope to all Canadians. We want our country to take the necessary steps from denial to acknowledgement, from tolerance to commitment, from inequality to the sharing of power, from institutionalized violence to zero tolerance of violence.

No hesitation can be tolerated. Women have spoken; women have written; women have acted. What will be the response? Our ultimate goal is the year 2000.

Now it is your turn. We urge you to lend your strengths, your hearts, your talents and your energy to changing the landscape which has kept the violence in place for so long. We have a rare opportunity to work together to implement real change, to create a society where there will be safety and equality for women. We can and we must do it now for ourselves, for our sisters and for our daughters.

Pat Freeman Marshall
Co-chair

Marthe Asselin Vaillancourt
Co-chair

PART ONE

EXECUTIVE SUMMARY

THE PANEL BACKGROUND AND MANDATE

The Canadian Panel on Violence Against Women came about as a direct result of the efforts of a small group of women who inspired a coalition of more than 30 national groups, including women's groups, who came together to urge the Prime Minister to establish a Royal Commission on violence against women. The coalition was formed on the eve of the 20th anniversary of the 1970 Royal Commission on the Status of Women and in the aftermath of the massacre of 14 women engineering students in Montreal at Ecole Polytechnique on December 6, 1989.

Ironically, the 1970 Royal Commission while expansive in its range of subject matter did not mention the subject of violence against women a reflection, unquestionably, of the longstanding curtain of silence which surrounded women and their abuse. The coalition aimed to pull back that curtain.

The coalition initiated a campaign which resulted in petitions of 26,000 names and letters. Two provincial premiers, mayors from across the country and four provincial ministers responsible for the status of women supported the call for a Royal Commission. Together with the membership and interests represented by the coalition, the level of support represented over 10 million Canadians.

Prior to the massacre in Montreal, the federal parliamentary Standing Committee on Health and Welfare, Social Affairs, Seniors and the Status of Women established the Sub-committee on the Status of Women in June, 1989. In June, 1991 the Sub-committee presented its findings in a report title, *The War Against Women*. The Report included a recommendation that the federal government take a leadership role and work with women's groups across the country and the provinces to establish a Royal Commission on violence against women.

In the speech from the Throne in May, 1991 the Prime Minister announced the creation of a panel to inquire into the problem of violence against women and to develop solutions, and in August 1991 the Honourable Mary Collins, Minister Responsible for the Status of Women, introduced the appointed members of The Canadian Panel on Violence Against Women.

At the outset, the Panel comprised two fulltime co-chairs and seven part-time members. As well, a four member Aboriginal Circle was created which was to have filled an advisory function. However, the Circle's role expanded to full participation in the Panel's work in order to bring attention to the unique needs and circumstances of status and non status Aboriginal women, including those living on reserve and the 43 per cent who live off reserve, as well as Inuit and Métis women.

In addition, a 23 member Advisory Committee was appointed to provide advice and input to the Panel and to be a link between the Panel and women's organizations. The Advisory Committee met on 5 occasions during the life of the Panel, including a joint meeting with representatives of national women's organizations.

The role of the Canadian Panel on Violence Against Women has been to engage Canadians in a dialogue on violence against women in an interactive, responsive grass roots manner, with the aim of producing solid recommendations for preventive action, immediate intervention and long term implementation. The nature of its work meant that few of the Panel's sessions were formal, no court reporters were present, and dialogue between participants and Panel members was encouraged. The Panel functioned at arm's length from the federal government with its own Secretariat.

---

* *Throughout the Executive Summary, the voices of women who spoke to the Panel are highlighted in italicized purple print. Where the voices of several women appear together, the testimonies of particular women are separated by the symbol for women.*

Although *The War Against Women* recommended a Royal Commission, it was decided that informal proceedings were more suited to the grass roots approach of the Panel's work: women who came forward were assured low key, private and secure surroundings such as community halls, transition houses, Indian band offices, women's shelters and public libraries. This decision was supported by women experience in the field with whom the Panel conducted some pre-consultation meetings.

The following mandate was given to the Panel:

- to examine violence against women in all its forms and document the incidence, root causes, effects and links between the various forms;

- to identify and define the violence from the perspective of women's experiences;

- to heighten public awareness of violence against women;

- to seek solutions, relating to the root causes of violence, with an emphasis on prevention; and,

- to produce recommendations for ending violence against women in all public and private sectors of Canadian society and to create a National Action Plan with time frames for federal government action.

In her public address at the launch of the Panel, the Honourable Mary Collins said:

> "Violence against women must come to an end. It is unacceptable in any form in Canadian society. 'Zero tolerance' must be our goal. We must seek out the underlying causes of this violence and devise solutions which will prevent it from occurring in the future. Only through prevention can we achieve long term, permanent solutions."

The Panel's work consisted of two phases. In Phase I, the Panel undertook a very extensive consultation process, the results of which are documented in greater depth in the Panel's Progress Report released in August 1992.
From January to the end of May 1992, the Panel travelled to all parts of Canada, including the Yukon and Northwest Territories, to consult with more than 4,000 people in 139 communities.

Eighty four per cent of the people who came forward were women, 16 per cent were men. In five months, the Panel members, working in small teams, attended a total of 441 events over the course of seven tours.

The Panel resolved to give a voice to women either silenced or never heard before. It took great effort to go beyond the service workers and helping professions to reach individual women who had not been, and likely never would be, part of any organization or assistance network.

During these consultations and in the ensuing months, the Panel received nearly 700 submissions from individuals and organizations. The subject areas of the submissions included personal testimonies, discussion papers and reports on the causes of violence against women, descriptions or critiques of community programs, and policy recommendations for the Panel's consideration.

In Phase II of the Panel's work, the Panel members carefully considered the enormous quantity of personal testimony, recommendations and research information accumulated by the Panel during Phase I. A number of formal and information consultation events were convened by the Panel for the purpose of discussing specific topics related to violence against women with particular groups of women in Canada. The formal events are listed in Appendix B. During Phase II the Panel focussed primarily on distilling what it had heard and learned in Phase I, and on developing the National Action Plan we were mandated to produce.

In addition to the consultations, the Panel initiated research work which enabled it to draw upon the experience, knowledge and analytical insights of women's organizations. Data from the Panel consultations was complemented by a review of the considerable body of research and documentation on violence against women already undertaken by women's organizations, academics and governments. Neither the nature nor the term of the Panel's mandate permitted the conduct of primary research. However, researchers were contracted to consolidate work already done in less thoroughly examined subject areas such as violence against women of colour, refugee women, domestic workers, and women living in rural settings, among others.

We partially funded a Toronto-based study of violence against women, The Women's Safety Project (discussed in more detail later on in this Executive Summary), which generated some important statistics on prevalence. As well, we distributed a survey through members of Parliament to their constitutents which provided another means for Canadians to share their experiences of violence and offer opinions about solutions.

It would be impossible in this relatively brief document to summarize all of the material contained in the Panel's Final Report. What must be done, however, is to communicate the Panel's perspective on violence against women as our approach underpins and explains both the overall scope and the specific measures set out in the National Action Plan which is Part Two of this document.

The Social Context of Violence

Every day in this country women are maligned, humiliated, shunned, screamed at, pushed, kicked, punched, assaulted, beaten, raped, physically disfigured, tortured, threatened with weapons and murdered. Some women are indeed more vulnerable than others, but all women, simply by virtue of their gender, are potential victims of violence. Moreover, the violence is often directed at them by those whom they have been encouraged to trust, those whom they are taught to respect, those whom they love. Violence against women cuts across all racial, social, cultural, economic, political and religious spectrums. While there is no question that violence may be conditioned by these factors, the fact remains that all women are at risk.

The voices of women throughout the Final Report are a sample of what we heard during our consultations across the country. Their words — unadorned, unedited — tell the story more effectively than volumes of explanation, exhortation and interpretation. The message is direct and urgent, carried by quotes throughout this text — voices of women of all ages, faiths, colour and class who have been there, are still there.

We know that Canadians have a sense that violence against women exists and that many women live with violence on a daily basis. However, we also know that Canadians do not have a real perception of the enduring repercussions of violence and how the experience and fear of violence affect the daily existence of women. There is no better way for people to appreciate these conditions than through the words of the women who have survived them.

The Panel's Final Report emphasizes that violence must be understood as a continuum that ranges from verbal insults through physical blows to murder. The voices we heard, the submissions we received and extensive research demonstrate the many dimensions of violence against women — physical, sexual, psychological, financial and spiritual. For many women, all these are part of their experience of violence.

Each individual experience of violence must be seen in a larger social context. An effective analysis of violence against women requires a framework, or a way of thinking about the issue which emphasizes that acts of violence are socially structured. Our approach rests on the premise that although individual men make individual choices to be, or not be, violent toward women, explanations that focus solely on individual characteristics and traits cannot account for the scope, proportion and dimensions of violence against women today and throughout history.

We call this focus a feminist lens through which violence against women is seen as the consequence of social, economic and political inequality built into the structure of society and reinforced through assumptions expressed in the language and ideologies of sexism, racism and class. We see this framework as an essential first step in working toward the goals of our National Action Plan.

While an examination and critique of gender inequality are often seen as the hallmarks of feminist thinking, a feminist approach also emphasizes the importance of recognizing women, not only as women, but as women of a particular class and race. These realities condition the lives of women in important and complex ways. A feminist analysis, if it is to be truly successful, must take the variations and the similarities among women into account. Our framework rests on the belief that violence is linked not only to the sexist nature of society, but also to the racism and class inequality upon which our society is based.

These social inequalities foster an atmosphere that tends to legitimize additional bases for social inequality, such as those linked to ability, age and sexual orientation. Any analysis of violence against women must include recognition of the complex ways in which inequality and power imbalances structure the lives of Canadian women. Only such an understanding can lead to ways of ending violence against women.

The feminist lens provides the Final Report with a particular focus on the social contexts in which Canadian women live — "taken for granted" places, settings and activities, families, schools, workplaces, political organizations and parties, religious institutions, community organizations, sports teams and expressions of popular culture including television, advertisements and magazines.

Women live in a social milieu textured by inequality, a reality that leaves them vulnerable to violence. As long as women have unequal access to choice and freedom, as long as women live with the fear of violence, their options will be restricted, their movements curtailed and their lives vitally affected.

Discussing violence against women is a balancing act. While we want to portray a sense of the truly horrific nature of violence against women and its implications, we do not want to portray women as the passive victims of violence or of male power. It has been women who have brought the issue of violence to the attention of the public, and it is women who have developed the essential analysis of violence against women. It is also almost exclusively women who work in transition houses, sexual assault centres, women's health clinics and crisis centres. These women are in the forefront of dealing with violence against women. Women in all capacities have assisted, informed, advocated for and protected other women throughout history. Women have been tireless in their work on legal reform and in their fight for increased funding and expansion of social and support services. Women are indeed the survivors of violence, not the passive victims. We hope our report moves Canadians to comprehend both the stark reality of violence against women and women's extraordinary efforts to change the nature of Canadian society.

VIOLENCE AGAINST WOMEN

Myths and misinformation surround violence against women. One of the most pervasive is the myth that places responsibility for violence on the victim rather than on the perpetrator: women provoke, tease and taunt men, invite their sexual advances and then push them away. Women annoy, disobey and confront, thus leading or contributing to the violence they encounter. They were wearing the wrong clothing, drank too much alcohol, walked alone at night, etc.

We flatly reject any analyses that place any degree of responsibility for violence on the women themselves no matter what their actions, appearance, demeanour or behaviour. Such assumptions detract from useful work and from the formulation of solutions. When Canadians realize the staggering levels of violence against women across this country, they too will reject individualized or specious explanations.

His fingers were digging into my arm, so I put my hand under his chin and pushed up hard. When I tried to get out of the car, he really blew up. "No fucking girl treats me like that!" Some nights I'd lie awake with crazy thoughts going around in my head: Maybe he has herpes or AIDS, and this was the only way he could get sex. Maybe I'm dying and I just don't know it.

♀♀♀

... he strangles me and takes me into the garage and tells me, "Now you're going to die." He has one hand on my throat and pulls back the other one to slap me in the face; with his fist in the air, he looks me straight in the eye and says, "You want to die?"

♀♀♀

The nightmare started right after the birth, which was very hard. He left me completely on my own and wouldn't let my mother help me. The fridge was completely empty most of the time, and he wouldn't let me ask my parents for help. My weight dropped to 83 pounds. When I asked my parents to give me some essential things for the baby, he kicked me in the coccyx, which had been injured by the particularly hard delivery. He took malicious pleasure in making a mess, in the bathroom, for example, where he spilt water all over the floor and told me I could wipe it up whenever I wanted. He ripped out the telephone line to cut me off from all assistance and potential help.

I called the police after my husband hit me. The officer arrived and said to me, "Would you mind shutting up and sitting down." He spoke to my husband even though I called him to help me.

♀♀♀

During the 27 years that I was married, I was continually abused both physically and emotionally. Twenty-two assault charges were laid against my husband, a few were dropped, but in most cases he was convicted. He never went to jail — he was merely sentenced to varying terms of probation. I left him many times and returned many times. I had no job and did not relish a welfare existence. To date, four years after I left him, there is still court action pending. My husband will probably win. He always has. Emotionally I am gaining strength although I am still afraid. Financially, I have nowhere to go but down. The money from the farm will not last long. I am too tired to fight anymore. Maybe some day I can go to sleep and never wake up.

VIOLENCE AGAINST WOMEN — DEFINITION AND DIMENSIONS

A shared definition of exactly what constitutes violence is crucial to the understanding of the sources and consequences of that violence. Although there has been a certain amount of debate on the subject, a proposed United Nations Declaration defines violence against women as

> ... any act of gender-based violence that results in, or is likely to result in, physical, sexual or psychological harm or suffering to women, including threats of such acts, coercion or arbitrary deprivation of liberty whether occurring in public or private life. [1]

The Declaration describes the persistence of violence against women as

> ... a manifestation of historically unequal power relations between men and women, which have led to domination over and discrimination against women by men and which have prevented women's full advancement. Violence against women is one of the crucial social mechanisms by which women are forced into a subordinate position compared to men. [2]

That violence against women is socially structured is the main tenet of our report. It is our belief that all social institutions, from the family through to the legal-judicial system, are characterized by unequal power relations between men and women. "Violence surpasses all other forms of abuse suffered by women. It occurs in private (families) and in public (pornography) and is the expression of the extreme limit of male dominance." [3] In the family, these power imbalances may express themselves in various ways, from an unequal division of household work or child care, to violent verbal, psychological, physical or sexual attacks. In the legal-judicial system, gender inequality is written into laws and manifests itself in charging policies and sentencing practices that fail to hold men accountable for their violent actions toward women.

While we recognize the extent to which violence against women is the outcome of inequality we also believe that individual acts of violence against women are individually willed.

> A man who exhibits violence verbally, psychologically, physically, sexually or financially toward his partner is not losing self-control; on the contrary, he is affirming his power, which he wants to preserve at all costs and which makes him neither monstrous nor sick. If he abuses his wife, it is because he has the privilege and the means to do so. [4]

Men who are violent bear sole responsibility for their violent actions. By systematically using power and control to override the will of their victims they make conscious choices including their choice of victim, the places and circumstances of their violence and the degree of force they use. Abusive behaviour cannot be explained away by loss of control or unfavourable circumstances. Problems within relationships, stress, alcohol, anxiety, depression and unemployment may contribute to violence against women, but they are neither acceptable excuses nor root causes. Other people under the same circumstances choose not to harm women. Removing these conditions alone will not end male violence against women.

In a society whose very structure condones male violence, all men, whether or not they are violent, derive substantial benefit from its institutionalization. The advantage may be as meagre as receiving preferential treatment in a group discussion, or as grand as avoiding competition with women for a job. The threat of violence also keeps women in unwanted relationships with men, defines the social situations and locations that women frequent, restricts women's activities in the workplace and undermines their potential for self-expression and self-confidence. All women pay the price of male violence: while not every woman has directly experienced violence, there are few who do not fear it and whose lives are not in some way affected and restricted by its pervasive presence in our society. [5]

NAMING VIOLENCE AGAINST WOMEN

All forms of male violence against women we refer to as woman abuse. The term "family violence" was widely used in both research literature and service delivery in the 1970s and 1980s to describe what actually constitutes abuse of women — not family. Although the home may be the most dangerous place for girls and women, the term is misleading and inaccurate.

The term "family violence" is a euphemism for violence against women and children, and it works to protect men .... Men's abuse is a social problem — they don't change because they don't have to.

Like many of the people from whom we heard, we choose to name the violence accurately. Using the term family violence to describe what is overwhelmingly violence against women obscures the facts. Further, we feel that the term "family violence" masks the huge spectrum of violence that women encounter outside their intimate relationships or families. We focus on the damage violence does to women and not its effects on the family institution.

IDENTIFYING DIMENSIONS OF VIOLENCE

For the purposes of analysis, we have divided violence against women into five dimensions: physical, sexual, psychological, financial and spiritual. In an intimate relationship, these dimensions may be experienced as a progression. In other cases, the experience may be of a single dimension of violence, or a combination of several. For these reasons, when enumerating the different dimensions, we have chosen to illustrate both the random and the escalating nature of violence.

Physical violence, the most obvious, can range from pushing and shoving, to hitting, beating, torture and murder. Sexual violence — i.e., any form of non-consensual sexual activity ranging from unwanted sexual touching to rape — must be clearly distinguished from intimate sexual contact which is mutual and consensual in nature. Because sexual violence often takes place within socially sanctioned relationships — marriage, dating, live-in partnerships as well as familial, parental and work relationships — its identification and disclosure are more difficult.

Psychological violence encompasses various tactics to undermine a woman's self-confidence, such as taunts, jeers, insults, abusive language, threats of physical violence or isolation. The deliberate withholding of various forms of emotional support may also be used. In relationships where children are present, men may also taunt women regarding their suitability as mothers or feed lies to the children to undermine their love and attachment to their mothers. The Panel heard many instances of men spreading lies about their partners at their places of work, in the community and in social groups or denying them the use of the car and telephone and monitoring their mail. Some men use various emotional and psychological tactics to ensure that a woman cuts ties with her nuclear and extended families. Such actions erode and eventually destroy a woman's social relationships, leaving her isolated and vulnerable.

Women are also the victims of financial violence. Male partners and/or family members may deny women access to employment opportunities outside the home or to other avenues for gaining some financial independence, such as part-time work or taking care of children in their own homes. Men may withhold or maintain control over all or substantial amounts of money. Women are sometimes cheated out of their inheritance, employment or other income. This may involve denying women access to financial records and knowledge about investments, income or debt. Senior women are often the victims of financial abuse.

Spiritual abuse erodes or destroys an individual's cultural or religious beliefs through ridicule or punishment. Perhaps one of the most heinous examples of such abuse was the establishment of the residential school system which resulted in the uprooting of Aboriginal children to be "educated" in the white educational system. Such education was founded upon the destruction of Aboriginal languages, traditions and beliefs in favour of the dominant culture. Residential schools provide a striking example of the interrelationships between racism, sexism and violence. Another example of spiritual violence is the exclusion of women from key positions in some religious institutions.

Categorizing dimensions of violence is helpful for discussion purposes and to underscore the breadth and depth of brutality women have endured and continue to endure. It is not so cut-and-dried in real life. The reality is that in many instances the violence women suffer entails a combination of all these dimensions. A woman who has been battered by her partner may have been raped by him, verbally maligned, psychologically scarred and financially deprived as well.

PREVALENCE OF VIOLENCE AGAINST WOMEN IN CANADA

Almost daily, newspapers, and radio and television broadcasts carry chilling reports of women harassed, women terrorized, women raped, women shot, women bludgeoned, women killed — almost always by men. So prevalent are these events that they have been described by one parliamentary committee as a "war against women." [6] And the accounts that reach the media are only a fraction of the events that never get reported, that remain invisible.

Despite a wealth of research in the area, we have only educated estimates of the prevalence of violence against women in Canada today. No matter what methodology is used, the figures are consistently alarming and, most researchers point out, underestimate the incidence of violence.

This is not likely to change because, for many women, there are good reasons not to disclose their experiences of violence. Fear of reprisal is the principal one: they keep silent often knowing from past experience that they will pay a painful price if they speak out. Another reason for silence is shame. Many women feel degraded by the abuse and cannot bear to talk about the violence they survive with family, friends or even strangers.

Some women have come to believe that they are somehow responsible for the violence. Their self-esteem has been so eroded that they consider themselves failures for not achieving the "domestic bliss" for which women are held responsible. The risk of being judged by those around them is often intolerable. Other women fear having to leave the relationship if they disclose its violent nature. Some are still hoping for change in the man they love; others know they cannot manage to support themselves and their children if they do leave.

Another major reason some women will not tell is that they know they will not be believed. Too often this has been reinforced by denial among friends and family members who have seen the signs of abuse and have done nothing to help. And tragically, some women cannot tell because they cannot remember. To survive they have blocked out memories too painful to recall. The best and most scientific methods of data collection cannot overcome these enforced silences.

Current research is also limited by its exclusion of many Canadian women. In particular, very little has specifically focused on the experiences of Inuit and Aboriginal women, women of colour, immigrant and refugee women, rural, poor or homeless women, women with disabilities, women with low literacy skills and lesbians. Also, much research is carried out in French and/or English, thereby excluding women who do not understand or speak these languages.

HIGHLIGHTS OF THE FINDINGS OF THE
WOMEN'S SAFETY PROJECT

The following information is based on 420 in-depth interviews with women between the ages of 18 and 64.

SEXUAL ABUSE OF GIRLS (AGE 16 AND UNDER)

- **More than one half (54 percent) of the women** had experienced some form of unwanted or intrusive sexual experience before reaching the age of 16.

- **24 percent of the cases** of sexual abuse were at the level of forced or attempted forced sexual intercourse.

- **17 percent of women** reported at least one experience of incest before age 16.

- **34 percent of women** had been sexually abused by a non-relative before age 16.

- **43 percent of women** reported at least one experience of incest and/or extrafamilial sexual abuse before age 16.

- **96 percent of perpetrators** of child sexual abuse were men.

SEXUAL ABUSE OF WOMEN (AGE 16 AND OVER)

- **51 percent of women** have been the victim of rape or attempted rape.

- **40 percent of women** reported at least one experience of rape.

- **31 percent of women** reported at least one experience of attempted rape.

- Using the Canadian Criminal Code definition of sexual assault (this includes sexual touching): **two out of three women**, have experienced what is legally recognized to be sexual assault.

- **81 percent of sexual assault cases** at the level of rape or attempted rape reported by women were perpetrated by men who were known to the women.

PHYSICAL ASSAULT IN INTIMATE RELATIONSHIPS

- **27 percent of women** have experienced a physical assault in an intimate relationship.

- **In 25 percent of the cases,** women who were physically assaulted reported that their partners explicitly threatened to kill them.

- **In 36 percent of the cases,** women reporting physical assault also reported that they feared they would be killed by their male intimate. Typically, women reported that the fury and violence exhibited during attacks made them fear for their lives.

- **50 percent of the women** reporting physical assault also experienced sexual assault in the context of the same relationship.

- **All of the physical assaults on women** were perpetrated by male intimates.

WOMEN'S SAFETY PROJECT

In the absence of nationally tabulated statistics on the full scope of violence against women, the Panel partially funded a community-based study in Toronto, the Women's Safety Project.[7] This work, already in progress when the Panel was appointed, was designed to overcome many of the usual limitations of studies on violence against women: subjects were randomly selected, the study took place in a centre with a diverse population and the large sample of 420 women meant more accurate statistics. In-depth interviews were conducted on a one-to-one basis by trained interviewers, and safety plans for the women interviewed were put in place. In addition, the project authors, Melanie Randall and Lori Haskell, brought with them an extensive knowledge of the topic. A detailed summary of the findings of the Women's Safety Project report to the Panel is found in Appendix A of the Final Report . The highlights of the project's findings in the chart on page 11 underscore what many women's groups have known for years: the statistics of violence against women in Canada have been thoroughly skewed by silence.

In the Safety Project interviews, women were asked about a wide range of abuse in a variety of contexts and relationships, from being followed or chased on the street, to receiving an obscene phone call, being sexually harassed at work, being sexually assaulted and/or raped as a child or adult or being physically assaulted and/or beaten in an intimate relationship.

When all kinds of sexual violation and intrusion are considered, 98 percent of women reported that they personally experienced some form of sexual violation. This finding, in particular, clearly supports our assertion that violence against women affects virtually all women's lives. Such violence is the product of a society where men's violence is often presented as a form of entertainment, either as a sensation in the media or glorified in movies and on television. Awareness of the possibility of sexual violence exists in the consciousness of most women. In a 1993 Maclean's -CTV poll, 55 percent of women in Canada reported that they are afraid to walk the streets of their community alone at night. [8]

HUMAN, SOCIAL AND FINANCIAL COSTS OF VIOLENCE AGAINST WOMEN

The statistics of the preceding section indicate the extent of the violence against women but not the costs. The human costs — the central concern of the Panel — are impossible to quantify. We heard from women whose lives have been totally disrupted by violence, from women who had to move away from friends, family, jobs, educational opportunities just to survive, from women whose lives have been wrenched asunder by exposure to a host of violent men — fathers, grandfathers, brothers, boyfriends, uncles, husbands, lovers, acquaintances and strangers.

The enormous emotional toll of these relationships defies any accounting mechanism. Some women are unable to sustain relationships over the long term, and some are afraid to leave their homes, paralyzed by an experience of violence which keeps them hostage. Some must witness the legacy of a violent relationship as it affects their own children; some cannot support themselves because they are unable to keep a job due to stress and the psychological toll of their experiences. A Quebec study [9] compared the health of a sample group of women and children who had left a violent environment with women and children of a comparable group who had not experienced violence. It concluded that:

> The health of these women and their children was distinctly different from that of the general population, and they were affected first of all by problems of mental health ... women who have escaped violence for good are in better mental health, but this separation is above all beneficial for the children. These findings [of the study] suggest that the improved health of abused women, and especially that of their children, is conditional on their breaking away from the violent spouse. [10]

Women from violent relationships were five times more likely to exhibit psychological problems than women from the control group. In total, 45.5 percent of women from violent relationships exhibited such problems compared with only 9.4 percent of the women from the control group. [11]

Years of abuse or a single incident can cause nightmares for years and make physical contact or a healthy sexual relationship impossible. These costs are personal, substantial and potentially overwhelming. For some women, killing their abusive husbands was the final outcome in the cycle of violence. In Montreal, between 1982 and 1986, three percent of all male homicides were committed by their female partners. In almost every case, the woman was in immediate or imminent danger of physical violence and was living in an abusive situation.

In at least half the killings of women in the same period, the men committed the murders because they could not accept the women leaving them; in other cases they committed the murder as revenge for having "lost control" over their wives' lives; in at least one case out of four, the men had previously used violence against their female partners. [12]

The physical costs are also tremendous. Broken limbs, scars, lacerations, cuts, bruises, internal damage, brain damage, reproductive damage including the inability to bear children, these are but a few of the physical costs that women endure. Some women pay with their lives. A Quebec study shows that approximately 20 percent of women admitted for emergency surgery are victims of violence. [13] Battering accounts for one in every four suicide attempts by women. Compared with women who have not been abused, 40 percent more battered women report that they use drugs to sleep; 74 percent more use drugs to relieve anxiety. [14]

The monetary costs of violence against women are hard to calculate. An experience of violence puts a woman in touch with a variety of institutions. The lack of co-ordination among these institutions means it is difficult, if not impossible, to follow someone through the process or to

make an accurate accounting of the human and financial costs of violence against women. However, some very obvious conclusions are possible.

Every misdiagnosis or missed diagnosis adds significant costs to the health care system. There are thousands of women in Canada who have received inappropriate medical care after an episode of violence. We heard of terrible hardship and suffering resulting from often-inappropriate treatment and tortuous incarcerations in hospitals. In many instances, these were the result of a misdiagnosis that led to dangerously inappropriate medications, use of strait-jackets and other questionable medical treatments.

Other costs to the Canadian medical system, correct diagnosis or not, include the cost of prescription drugs such as anti-depressants, sleeping pills and painkillers; the cost of appointments with physicians, emergency treatment, hospital stays, ambulance services; and the cost of rehabilitative services such as physiotherapy or occupational therapy. The fact is the financial toll of violence against women is entirely preventable, an important recognition for a health care system already severely overburdened.

For women survivors of violence, work-related costs include time off without pay due to the results of injury and psychological trauma. They may also include the cost of using employment-based counselling services or sick leave, and in some instances it may even be necessary to leave a job altogether. Victims of violence may not be able to concentrate on work and may exhibit decreased productivity. Such costs accrue, not only to the women involved, but also to their employers, insurance companies, all levels of government, disability pension programs, workers, criminal compensation programs, etc.

The financial costs of violence against women are not restricted to health care and work-related costs; they also reverberate through the criminal justice system. Additional police resources, victims' treatment costs, insurance claims and court costs all add up. In cases where convictions and sentencing take place, the correctional system bears the costs of detention, incarceration, probation and parole. In some instances both defendants and plaintiffs use legal aid, a further cost to the system.

The cost benefits of violence prevention and effective programs for offenders have not been clear to many because such costs have never been realistically or comprehensively tabulated in Canada. Even a rough estimate of the cost associated with one crime of violence against a woman provides some appreciation of the need to prevent violence from happening in the first place. The costs of one sexual offence, where the offender serves three years in prison, can be very conservatively estimated at more than $200,000. The prison custodial cost alone would be approximately $50,000 per year for three years. Added to this would be the costs of police investigation, pre-trial and court processes, assessment, parole hearings, offender programs and after-prison care as well as some services to the victim.

And then there are the social costs of violence against women, which include an expensive range of social services and supports which must be maintained on an ongoing and emergency basis. Services for children need to factor in the costs of foster homes and additional child care workers. The educational system has to provide child welfare services over and above those of education, such as school crisis counsellors, tragic events teams, special education classes for children with learning disabilities resulting from violence, as well as special programs and educational initiatives on violence. Communities, municipalities, provincial and federal governments must bear the costs of transition houses, second-stage housing, mental health clinics, shelter programs, educational campaigns, special services for victims of violence, sexual assault centres and programs for violent men.

While we have not been able to attach monetary sums to all the costs outlined above, we know they are profound. Instead of devoting such a large percentage of already limited monetary resources to activities in *response* to the consequences of violence against women, would it not be much wiser to direct the funds to programs aimed at preventing the perpetuation of violence and to social change?

LOOKING THROUGH A FEMINIST LENS

The analysis in this report draws on a specific way of thinking about violence against women. Rather than focusing on the violent actions of individual men, our approach looks at the problem in a much broader social context. We are asking: What is it about our present and past social organization that fosters and supports violent actions on the part of men toward women?

Our approach is not new. We have taken a feminist approach reflecting work already done at the grass-roots level. In the pages which follow we will demonstrate how looking through a feminist lens enables us to see how gender, race and class oppress women and how these forms of oppression are interrelated and interconnected.

PATRIARCHY AND VIOLENCE

Violence against women, both now and in the past, is the outcome of social, economic, political and cultural inequality. This inequality takes many forms, but its most familiar form is economic. [15]

Day-to-day economic inequality, unequal political power, unequal protection under the law and unequal access to justice for women are all supported and perpetuated at the level of ideas. Language, myths, symbols, notions and beliefs about the superiority of men over women bolster the existing social structure and maintain women's inequality.

Understanding the concept of patriarchy is essential to our analysis of the nature of gender inequality and its impact on the vulnerability of women to violence, and of our society's tolerance of male violence against women.

DIMENSIONS OF INEQUALITY

Canada ranks second among nations (to Japan) on the Human Development Index compiled by the United Nations. [16] However, when the Index is adjusted for gender disparities, Canada drops to 11th place overall. While the statistical basis upon which the UN compiles its Human Development Index is open to debate the following statistics illustrate the objective realities of gender inequality Canadian women face every day.

1. The average annual wage of women full-time workers in 1991 was $ 26,842. For men it was $38,567. [17]

2. The average wage of women increased by 14 % in the decade of the 1980s, while that of men remained constant. However by 1990, despite a decade of employment equity and increased educational attainment and work experience among women, women's earnings were still just 60.3 % those of men. [18]

3. Three out of four earners in the 10 lowest paying occupations are women. Eight out of ten earners in the highest paying occupations are men. [19]

4. The lowest average employment income in 1990 was for child care occupations at $ 13,518. [20]

5. The average income for female lone parent families in 1990 was $ 26,500. For male lone parent families it was $ 40,792. There were 165,245 male lone parent families and 788,400 female lone parent families in 1990. [21]

6. In 1989, only 7 % of all full professors at Canadian universities were women. In engineering and applied sciences women accounted for only 15 % of lecturers and instructors and just 1 % of full professors. Even in education faculties, only 15 % of full professors were women. [22]

7. 11 % of women in 2 parent families with pre-school children missed work in 1991 for family reasons. Only 2 % of men in these families had absences from work for family reasons. [23]

8. On average, women who work outside the home for pay spend almost an hour and a half more per day on unpaid household work, including domestic work, primary child care and shopping, than do men — 3.2 hours per day on average over a 7-day week compared with 1.8 hours per day for men. [24]

9. Four times as many women as men reported that 4 out of 5 domestic responsibilities were mostly theirs. Women said they had the main responsibility for household shopping, cleaning inside the home, looking after ill children and taking children to activities. Men said they had primary responsibility only for "cleaning outside the home". [25]

10. 42 % of women household maintainers (i.e. the person responsible for mortgage, rent, taxes and upkeep) own their dwelling, compared with 70 % of male household maintainers. [26]

11. Elderly unattached women are among the poorest Canadians. But, while the percentage of these women living in poverty has gone down since 1980, an increasing proportion of all low income elderly people are women. [27]

12. In 1991-92, all levels of government expended $ 1.876 billion on adult correctional services. On an average day, there were 25,712 prisoners serving a custodial sentence. Women accounted for just 1,254 or 9 % of all provincial prisoners, and only 354 or 3 % of all federal inmates. [28]

13. Women account for 10 % of all persons charged with violent crimes and 20 % of those charged with property crimes. [29]

14. Breast cancer is the leading cause of death for Canadian women aged 35-54 and the leading cause of death from cancer for women aged 30-74. Less than 1 % of health care research funds are spent on breast cancer. [30]

THE PATRIARCHAL SOCIETY

Patriarchy in its wider meaning is:

> The manifestation and institutionalization of male dominance over women and children in the family and the extension of male dominance over women in society in general. It implies that men hold power in all the important institutions in society and that women are deprived of access to such power. It does not imply that women are either totally powerless or totally deprived of rights, influence and resources, but certainly women as a group have less power, less influence and fewer resources than men. [31]

In the social structures and dynamics of society, women and men have gender-specific roles in the power structure which, among other things, legitimize men's authority to be violent toward women. [32] Some men consider domination and control of women as their right; using violence when they see fit is not challenged. This in turn leads to widespread tolerance of male violence at both the individual and institutional levels.

The treatment of women, their labour, their reproductive capacity and their sexuality as commodities is certainly not just a product of modern industrial and capitalist society; it has been that way since long before the creation of Western civilization. Over time, women became a resource and a form of property acquired and controlled by men.

Today, the modern state and its supporting bureaucracy have broadened the locus of power from the patriarch in the family to a patriarchal state that reflects and sustains gender inequality in a variety of ways and locations in the social structure. [33] In concert, the patriarchal family model and the patriarchal state help to sustain inequality among women and men. This major enduring theme does not deny that most women have established greater relative equality over time, but they have done so within the context of a patriarchal society. The nature of gender relations and inequality in society can be better understood through an elaboration of the concept of heterosexism, a set of ideas about men and women and the relationship between them.

HETEROSEXISM

Heterosexism is the assumption that a woman's life will be organized around and defined in relation to a man. It falsely presumes that all women will marry and have children, and that all worthy paths for women lead to marriage and motherhood. Opposition to heterosexism is often unfairly cast as an attack on the institutions of marriage and motherhood. In reality, opposition to heterosexism supports women's equality. It upholds a woman's right to be defined as an autonomous, independent person rather than being defined only in relation to men and children. It recognizes the diverse roles a woman plays in life and frees her to attach priorities to these roles as she sees fit. It supports a woman's right to choose her love partner with freedom, and it calls for a transformation of societal structures that support all freely chosen relationships.

Canadian society is organized around compulsory heterosexuality. Our culture and societal institutions function as if the primary role for women is that of wife and mother caring for her husband and bearing and nurturing children. In the ideal, she is the archetypal madonna: demure, slight, beautiful, chaste, deferential, passive, co-operative, alluring and servile. These feminine attributes prepare her to marry and be relegated to the private domain of the family. Her greatest assigned values are her reproductive capacity and her commitment to her family. Her domestic labour remains unpaid; her paid work remains underpaid.

In antithesis to the ideal woman, the ideal man is the protector and the breadwinner. He is seen to be best equipped for that role if he is bold, strong, powerful, active, competitive, virile and in command. These masculine characteristics have high value in the private realm of the family where he is seen to be the head of the household, and in the public spheres of commerce, law and politics. He is presumed to be a careerist first and a husband second. His masculine qualities are valued highly and are well rewarded in the marketplace. He carries these qualities with him into the public world where they become the core philosophy and where structures are crafted to suit the male experience.

We continue to live with the legacy of these archetypes. Despite modern reality, our institutions and social conventions are all constructed in a manner that limits choices for women in an effort to force them to conform to the role of wife and mother. Families, religion, politics, media and education are all organized around the concept of heterosexism and consistently reinforce and re-create the ideal by rewarding those who most closely conform to it and by punishing those who dare to be different. Hence the tomboy is tamed, the outspoken woman is silenced, the prostitute is cast out. Heterosexism is evident in worries about appearance, eating disorders, reluctance to participate in sports and hiding academic achievements to avoid appearing too smart or too successful.

The quest is supported in educational institutions that schedule dances instead of group social events, in religious institutions that perpetuate the ideology of male superiority and female inferiority, in workplaces that undervalue and underpay women, and in popular culture that sustains sexist assumptions about women.

The imbalance of power inherent in the masculine and feminine sex roles takes on greater significance when we look at the dynamics of male violence against women. Generally men are in control and women are controlled by them. Men are independent; women are dependent on them. When men choose violence as a means to control women, women have little power to withstand the violence. Even men who do not actively use violence against women often tolerate it by other men.

The mechanisms through which male violence can be challenged are also infused with the belief in the male right to rule women. Heterosexism is imbedded in all state institutions that women are likely to call upon — the police, the justice system and religious institutions. In these structures, women, particularly if they do not fit the idealized image of wife and mother, have little influence and power. They are often not believed, they are blamed for their own suffering and are urged to try harder.

If women attempt to gain economic independence to lessen their vulnerability, they come up against structural obstacles. The labour force remains organized around the heterosexist ideal, presuming women to be married, to maintain primary responsibility for the home and to care for children, despite their labour force participation. They are usually paid less than men, primarily found in lower status and more "servile" jobs, and frequently relegated to part-time positions with fewer benefits and pension rights. For women who are participating in the labour force or want to participate, inadequate child care can be a major problem.

Love relationships between men and women are celebrated and sanctified while same sex relationships are denied and reviled. Pension plans, health care schemes and insurance policies discriminate against them. Less apparent, but real nonetheless, are the difficulties faced by women who choose to remain unmarried or who choose not to have or cannot have children. They are consistently asked why not and are looked upon as unfortunate or somehow deviant. Lone parents, most of whom are women, lack societal supports.

On the surface, women who live within heterosexist boundaries seem better off. Many, without doubt, garner privileges, such as access to male resources, a husband's protection from other men and legitimacy for children born of the relationship. But these are all derivative benefits. The man continues to be the primary source of support, defines the terms of protection and gives the children his name. Power is his to wield as he wishes. In this arrangement the woman remains in a state of dependency on the man, vulnerable to his will.

If women choose to speak out against heterosexism and its inherent inequality, to resist it, to expose the male violence it supports, they are considered "shrill" and unwomanly and often face violence for doing so. Heterosexism is one of patriarchy's strongest and most insidious tools. It allows society to cast aside women's experience and construct a society on models of what patriarchy wants her to be, not who she really is or could be.

Sexism and sexist assumptions are also expressed in laws; in religious rituals; in economic practices; in myths and stories; in children's games, toys and reading materials; and in scores of additional places in society.

Patriarchy is not just a central concept in feminist analysis. For many women it is also a daily reality — the most violent and profound expression of patriarchal power sits at their dinner tables every evening and sleeps in their beds at night. Women who have experienced violence at the hands of their husbands and intimate partners, or their fathers, brothers, uncles or grandfathers, can speak all too clearly about male power; they have self-images, bruises, cuts, lacerations and broken bones that speak of their understanding of the patriarchal family. Although we recognize that positive aspects of family life can and do exist, for some women the reality is in stark contrast to the mythical images most Canadians hold dear.

It is ironic that, while separate and distinct from the public world of work and politics, the family is a private realm where men still dominate and exercise the same control they wield in the public arena. Traditional family relations also confer certain "conjugal rights" upon men. Exclusive and unlimited sexual access to women by men has been a cornerstone of the family, a right often interpreted by some men to extend to their daughters, nieces and granddaughters. It was not until 1983 that a woman could charge her husband with rape in Canada. Until then, men had the legal right to rape their wives without fear of reprisal. [34]

Even after marriages break down, some men continue to exercise what they believe to be their proprietory rights to their wives and children. The best evidence we have of this belief in ownership is the incidence of "intimate femicide," murder of a woman by someone close to her. It is estimated that women who are separated from their spouses are five times more likely to be killed by their intimate partners than are other women. [35] Male anger and rage over the loss of their wives/ property apparently have no obvious counterpart in killings of men by female intimate partners. "If I can't have her, no one will have her" is the ultimate expression of the patriarchal family ideology.

Beliefs about privacy and the separation of "home" from the "other" world increase women's vulnerability. They permeate law and politics where violence in the home continues to be perceived as being beyond public reproach. Police officers shy away from "domestics," and implicitly or explicitly the message goes out that what happens in the family is not the business of the public.

We are taught, encouraged, moulded by and lulled into accepting a range of false notions about the family. As the source of some of our most profound experiences, it continues to be such an integral part of our emotional lives that it appears beyond criticism. Yet hiding from the truth of family life leaves women and children vulnerable. Many of us, including policy makers, legislators, law enforcement personnel, judicial officials, doctors and religious leaders, are afraid to examine the reality of power relations within the home. Many are quick to dismiss disclosures of psychological, physical or sexual abuse because such events depart so profoundly from our idealized images of family life. For many it is difficult to reconcile the conflicting images of father/husband as protector and father/husband as perpetrator of violence. As difficult as this process is, it is important that we confront the potential dangers of family life for women and children.

Patriarchy also finds expression in religious institutions that have a long history of domination, control and the exercise of absolute power. The theological domination of women by men omnipresent in religious teachings extends into the day-to-day practice of religious institutions. Women are excluded from many important religious ceremonies, segregated from some settings and forbidden to hold certain positions of power. Acceptable relationships between the sexes are governed by outdated notions about men, women and families. Some religions enslave women to procreation by prohibiting birth control and abortion. Some clergy have sexually abused women and children or advised women to stay in dangerous family situations.

Many religious institutions have, through both philosophy and practice, contributed to conditions that support violence against women in the home and in society.

Ultimately, patriarchal society is synonymous with the political, social, cultural and economic inequality of women. Unequal political power is exemplified by the current representation of women in political office and by the predominance of a male political culture that operates along lines of male privilege. Unequal sexual freedom sees women as objects of consumption in pornographic magazines and sees females taking almost total responsibility for birth control and being denied access to full choice around issues of childbearing. Unequal legal power is manifested in laws that do not adequately protect women and children as survivors of abuse and in regulations that discriminate against women in the determination of their immigrant and refugee status. Unequal social power keeps women silent, even in the midst of abusive treatment by partners, employers, doctors, social workers and clergy.

OTHER BASES OF INEQUALITY

Our report is about violence against women — violence women suffer because of their gender. But understanding the experience of violence requires understanding the combined impact of gender, race and class.

CLASS

Social inequality is the outcome of the interrelationship between the structures of economic power and the organization of male power in our society. This blending of power relations pervades all institutions. To truly understand women's inequality is to recognize how patriarchy and capitalism operate in separate ways but also combine forces to diminish their interests and realities further.

To see this interrelationship in action, one only has to examine women's low economic status and participation in the labour force as secondary workers. Society relies on women to provide a whole range of caring services to men, to children, to the sick and old, most often for free or for little money. This sexual division of labour repeats itself in the workplace with women continuing to be concentrated in only three occupational groups: clerical, service, and managerial and administrative. [35] Most of the positions in these groups offer low wages, limited benefits, low career mobility and very little union protection. [36]

Patriarchal-capitalistic relations also divide women themselves into groups with different levels of choice, power and control over all things in life, from the basics of what we eat, where we live and sleep, our education and jobs, to our encounters with government and the healthcare and legal systems. A woman's exposure to and experience of violence will also be textured by her socio-economic position. Access to financial resources will determine the level and the type of support, counselling, legal advice and other survival strategies at a woman's disposal.

RACE

Patriarchy is not fully revealed solely in terms of gender and class power differentials. Race power relations are involved as well. Just as Canadian ideologies, policies and social practices are structured around male and elite values and experiences, they are also rooted in the belief that white people have the right to dominate. Canadians are generally presumed to be white and this is the central reference point of all social institutions. Therefore racism is structural in nature and cannot be explained as the product of bad communication among individuals.

> ... racism is [not] merely a misunderstanding among people, a question of interpersonal relations, or an unchanging part of human nature. Racism, like sexism, is an integral part of the political and economic system under which we live.[37]

For women of colour, race, gender and class issues intersect very clearly in the labour market. Women are already seen as a secondary source of labour. Added to this are racist ideologies that "justify" low wages for women of colour and racist hiring practices that force many women of colour into low status jobs with poor working conditions. It is easy to see how two oppressions, gender and race, interlock in a way that forces class oppression into play. This is not simply a layering of three separate oppressions but a complex interplay of oppressions that results in compounded social inequality.

When a woman of colour experiences violence she experiences it as a simultaneous attack on both her gender and her race. From experience she knows that anger and hatred directed at both these aspects of her identity are real. When she calls upon systems to respond she cannot trust the response because she knows that she is calling upon systems that do not understand, value or incorporate her experience either as a woman or as a person of colour.

FROM ANALYSIS TO ACTION

The feminist lens reveals that while all women are at risk of male violence because of gender, their experiences of that violence are essentially informed by their race and class. So are the responses to their experiences. Building alliances across the issues that divide women will have to be given priority in the struggle to end violence against women. Patriarchy thrives on fragmentation and divisions. The existence of one oppression creates fertile conditions for the others. That is why all oppressions must be resisted together.

The action plan proposed by this Panel stresses the importance of eliminating the conditions that support patriarchy by emphasizing that gender equality and freedom from violence are equal and concurrent goals. However, we recognize that the experiences and the degree of violence are different for women of colour, for women of different races and different cultural and ethnic backgrounds, for poor and elderly women, for lesbians and for disabled women. Their particular experiences of inequality and of violence are the outcome of a society which devalues, marginalizes and discriminates against them. It is not the race, ethnicity, colour, age, physical ability or sexual orientation which make the lives of these women so different; it is how individuals and various sectors in the social structure react to the reality of these women that compounds their experiences of violence and inequality.

EXPERIENCING VIOLENCE ~ FORMS

The five dimensions of violence: sexual, physical, psychological, financial and spiritual. Rape, incest, date rape and unwanted sexual touching are forms of sexual violence; slapping, shoving, hitting, stabbing and murder are forms of physical violence; shouting, swearing, taunting, threatening, degrading and demeaning are forms of psychological violence; withholding money, diverting or embezzling funds and controlling money are forms of financial violence; degrading a woman's spiritual beliefs or withholding or limiting the means for her to practise her spirituality are forms of spiritual violence.

Violence, its short and long-term consequences, and the legal, moral and cultural sanctions attached to it, are best understood in the context of the relationships and settings in which it takes place.

Statistics clearly indicate that in the majority of cases of violence against women, the victims and the perpetrators are known to each other and share some sort of relationship. [39] Women victims are more likely to be the daughters, sisters, intimate partners, dates, employees and acquaintances of the perpetrators — not strangers. This flies in the face of the classical rape myth of a chaste woman beseiged by a stranger who jumps out from behind a bush on a darkly lit street. Most people can identify the crime and injury to the woman in such a scenario although some still question the woman's right to be on the darkly lit street; debate whether her clothes were too provocative and want to know if she was truly chaste.

There is a significantly different reaction to the rape of a woman who is in a relationship with the man who rapes her—any relationship. It appears that once any relationship exists, regardless of how casual it might be, men have come to believe in their right to dictate the terms.

The closer the relationship the greater the burden of proof of injury required by the woman. This leaves women in intimate relationships with men extremely vulnerable. We know that the law against rape in marriage is seldom used. This is not because women are not raped by husbands. On the contrary, the Women's Safety Project found that 25 percent of all rapes reported by women were committed by their husbands. Non-reporting confirms that women know, despite the current law, that reports of rape within marriage will fall on unwilling ears and reluctant justice. This is confirmed in all women's minds each time a woman is blamed for contributing to her own victimization by agreeing to have a drink with a man in his apartment, by inviting her date in for coffee, by agreeing to a midnight kiss. Such acts are deemed to signal agreement to a relationship, an agreement that nullifies a woman's right to say no to further physical intimacy.

In a relationship, society has given the man the power over a woman from the point of earliest acquaintance. Men exercise this power not only in intimate relationships and not only in sexual matters but in any social context where contact between women and men occurs.

The setting in which a relationship takes place can also amplify or diminish women's vulnerability to violence. Generally, the more private the setting the more vulnerable the woman. Again, while the peril of the street grips the attention of most people, it is the far less public venues that hold the greatest danger for women — the family home, the doctor's examining room, the boss's office. It is in these private spaces that men frequently exercise their power over women. Exposing the risks these settings present becomes the first step in reducing the danger.

In our Final Report we discuss several variants of violence against women in order to illustrate the infinite range of violence, and to show how violent acts against women are influenced by relationships and settings. The chart titled Forms of Violence helps describe the myriad forms of violence, the wide variety of possible perpetrator victim relationships and the range of settings where the violence can occur. It is the interrelationship of all three of these factors which together shape the experience of violence.

FORMS OF VIOLENCE

Dimensions:	*Forms include:*
Psychological	*shouting, swearing, taunting, threatening, degrading, demeaning, inducing fear, gender harassment, witnessing*
Sexual	*rape, incest, unwanted sexual touching, date rape, harassment*
Physical	*slapping, shoving, hitting, mutilation, stabbing, assault, murder*
Financial	*witholding, diverting, embezzling or controlling funds*
Spiritual	*degrading one's beliefs, witholding means to practice, forcing adherence to a belief system*

* Almost all forms of violence have a psychological impact on the victim and hence the psychological dimension of violence against women is omnipresent.

* Ritual abuse, abuse of trust, pornography, stalking and misuse of reproductive technologies are forms of violence often experienced as a combination of psychological, physical, spiritual and sexual dimensions.

PERPETRATOR-VICTIM RELATIONSHIPS

- stranger
- spouse
- intimate partner
- acquaintance
- friend
- date
- family member/relative
- coworker/colleague
- person in a position of trust or authority
  - e.g.
    - employer/supervisor
    - custodial worker
    - service provider
    - teacher
    - volunteer leader
- business person
- state (e.g. police, public servant, elected official, military)

- stranger
- spouse
- intimate partner
- acquaintance
- friend
- date
- family member/relative
- coworker/colleague

- employee
- woman in an institution
- patient/client
- student
- participant
- consumer
- citizen, immigrant, refugee

*   *Sometimes the perpetrator and victim have no relationship whatsoever   they are strangers to each other. However, in the majority of cases, the victim and perpetrator do know each other and have had some previous interaction. The nature of that interaction and the characteristics of the environment (interpersonal or institutional) within which it evolves help determine the nature of the abuse and its impact.*

SETTINGS

- house, apartment (one's own or someone else's)
- community: public space, street, park, transport system, restaurant, place of business, cultural, or recreation facility

- workplace
- institutions: school, hospital, place of worship, police station, residence

22

In the Final Report we purposely begin by looking at sexual violence enacted against women by strangers. While this is not the most common experience of sexual violence done to women, the past focus on family violence has often meant that sexual assault by strangers is ignored.

The Final Report discusses violence where the perpetrators are known to their victims, beginning with date rape and sexual violence in acquaintance or intimate relationships. We move on to discuss psychological violence in intimate relationships, an extremely common experience for women, less recognized in the literature and often not recognized at all in law. It is frequently the precursor to physical and sexual violence and has a devastating impact, sometimes undermining a woman's ability to escape other forms of violence. We then briefly look at physical violence in intimate relationships, forms that are more easily described and better recognized by society. This portion on violence in intimate relationships ends by addressing violence during pregnancy and examining women's fear of disclosing.

We go on to discuss child abuse. While our mandate did not call for such an examination, many women spoke of the damage done to them as girls and of the pain they still carry as a consequence of early victimization. We specifically focus on childhood sexual abuse, incest, female genital mutilation, the impact on girls and boys of witnessing abuse of their mothers and a preliminary investigation of the relationship between sexual abuse in childhood and revictimization in adulthood.

To illustrate the impact of the setting on the nature and response to violence, we then look at violence against women in the workplace — a setting that occupies much time and space in the lives of women and one that is so critical to a woman's ability to gain economic independence. We look at violence in the workplace generally and then at areas that pose unique and high risks to women, such as workplaces in nursing, education, domestic work and prostitution.

Our examination of forms of violence concludes with a discussion of several previously unacknowledged or underacknowledged forms of violence the Panel heard about during its consultations specifically, ritual abuse, stalking/criminal harassment, pornography, abuse of trust (both individual and institutional) and the potential for abuse through the misapplication of reproductive technology.

The voices of women who have survived the situations of violence described in this section of the Final Report speak for themselves.

I looked for help since 1979. I didn't get help. I stayed because I needed money. I was never good enough for my husband. He said I wasn't a good mother. When I was ill he denied me care. I threatened suicide he didn't care, he turned over and went to sleep .... Mental violence is as bad as physical violence. Before I was married I used to laugh and smile but my husband told me to stop. He tells me I can't have friends. He won't take me out. He keeps all the money. He tells me I'm stupid, ugly. He told me not to go to my daughter's graduation. When I told him he never liked her, he just turned up the volume on the TV .... He kicked my oldest daughter. He strapped my son. His behind was black and blue .... He expected to use me sexually but not to be a lover. He was rough.

♀ ♀ ♀

He tried to rape me. I told him that. He said he could do what he wanted because I was his wife .... I went to work but you lose control, you have to give the money to your husband, do all the housework and care for the kids ... and get physically and emotionally abused ....

♀ ♀ ♀

All of this is hard for me to speak of because I was raped by my boyfriend when I was in first year [university]. Even now, knowing it was not my fault, it is more intellectual than believing it for sure. I found the Women's Centre a really safe place to talk about it. It really affected my school work. I had to drop some of my courses, ones his friends were in. He is still on campus and when I see him, he looks at me to intimidate me, and I am a wreck for a week ....

♀♀♀

We all have a sense of invulnerability that allows us to get up in the morning and believe that bad things are not going to happen. That sense of invulnerability is destroyed after sexual assault; it's as though one is out in the world without a skin .... Loss of sense of safety, [and] increased fears are often misdiagnosed. Our basic assumption that if we do the right things in living, our lives will be OK is destroyed. Victims experience an absolute loss of trust in others and loss of sense of justice. Women's sense of self and sense of attachment are fractured. With that comes a profound loss of self-esteem and self-worth. Sexual violence violates the basic tenets of our being.

♀♀♀

I am an incest survivor. I was 18 months old when my father and two grandfathers started abusing me. I have multiple personalities and split memories. No one identified me as being an abuse victim or even as ill until a few years ago. Yet I had chronic pain and mental depression for years .... The hospitals and the church knew I was an incest victim. A hospital which knew of his sexual abuse of me sent him back to our family and left us with him ....

♀♀♀

One day, when I went out for a walk to relax, he followed me, and I had to return home. He then threatened me, saying that, no matter what the court's verdict might be, he would make sure he got justice, that he would find a way to go on legal aid and would fight back until I died, that he would never leave me in peace.

In the winter of 1991, he tripped me on a ski hill, and I almost skied off into the woods. Then he fled. Shortly afterward, when I was talking to a ski patroller, he went into a terrible fit of jealousy and threatened to punch us both out if he saw us together again.

♀♀♀

I was staff counsellor for... During that time the leader of the organization was having sex with almost every female client that came to us for counselling. The six women with whom I worked, including myself, would also work with these women after they had seen the "Boss." It was a very damaging situation. These women would have to work on the fact that this man was not really interested in them as a lover, or in even having a long- or short-term affair...they were simply being used by him... They came to him for help and they ended up with more problems.

♀♀♀

A woman working in a Prince Albert card shop who had to wear a promotional button saying "I Guarantee It" was dismissed when she refused to continue wearing the button because it invited sexual comments from male customers. By forcing the woman to wear the button, her employer was asking her to tolerate sexual harassment as a term and condition of her employment.

♀♀♀

While on my knees before him as he swung the poker down again and again so close to my head I could feel the wind from it on my face and hearing him say over and over "I could kill you, I could kill you," I envisioned my brains splashing forward onto the carpet. I willed him to do it, to end it all quickly, I waited on my knees for the blow that would set me free once and for all. I believed at that moment that this was my destiny, that the reason I had been placed on this Earth was to die at his hands and that his destiny was to kill me, that all roads led to here, to this particular moment.

My husband is also a great consumer and proponent of pornography. As a psychology professor he teaches students that there is no correlation between the consumption of pornography and the commission of violent or sexually degrading acts. Outside the classroom, however, and in the privacy of our home, I saw again and again how my husband mimicked with me what he saw in pornographic magazines and films. I believe in retrospect that the early beatings I received were sexual in nature and because they were committed in the so-called throes of passion or under the guise of uncontrollable male arousal, I did not even recognize the fact that I had been beaten.

♀ ♀ ♀

This was a generational cult that is linked and connected throughout the country. They use programming and brainwashing. I recently met a member from the past. She said two words to me and all I knew is that I felt like killing somebody. Cults are big business. They're involved with drugs, child porn, "snuff" movies and white slavery. It's hard to recall what happened and who is involved because you're fragmented into so many parts that you don't remember. I'm still trying to find out what they did to my head. It's different than other forms of sexual abuse, and nobody knows how to treat it. I live in fear. As long as I live dissociated, I live fine. But sometimes I'm frightened of the other parts of myself. Some of the people that did this to me are still alive and still in my life .... I'm dealing with great guilt because of some of the things I was made to do. It makes me so angry. A cousin warned me to stay away. He had changed his identity. You don't know how big it is. My real parents were murdered .... It makes me feel so helpless. I was involved in snuff movies and child porn.

EXPERIENCING VIOLENCE ~ POPULATIONS

All women are vulnerable to male violence; all women fear it at some level, are potential victims and suffer pain when struck or when verbally and psychologically tortured; all women look for ways to explain or understand what is happening to them; and all women want to be safe.

It would be false to assume that all women are equally at risk. Some women are more vulnerable than others. The degree of their exposure to violence is dictated not only by their individual circumstances but by broader factors including their class, culture, race, colour of skin, sexual orientation, physical and mental abilities, education, age, where they live, language and literacy levels. However, although such characteristics affect the intensity and degree of a woman's vulnerability to violence, they do not alter the conditions common to all women. It is not the "human" condition, rather it is the "woman" condition.

There are three factors underlying women's specific vulnerability:

- the widespread acceptance in our society of the subordination of women to men and the subordination of some women to other women;

- women's dependence on men and male systems; and

- isolation (physical, psychological and social) from the mainstream.

Within the hierarchy of a patriarchal society, the subordination of women renders them susceptible to violence everywhere: the home, the workplace, the streets and all public places, cities, rural areas and at the hands of family, institutions and service providers.

Women's dependence on men and male systems is economic, either through individual control, through inequities in the workplace, or through a controlling and dead-end social service system;

psychological, through societal pressure to link up with a man, any man; and physical, such as the dependence of women with disabilities on their caregivers or women from another culture and language who must rely on their husbands to communicate with the outside.

The third common factor, isolation, sets the scene for abuse of all forms. The isolation can be physical, social or psychological.

The discussion contained in Part Three of the Panel's Final Report, entitled Experiencing Violence – Populations, focusses on how these three major factors, which influence the vulnerability of all women, are intensified by the circumstances of individual populations. A subset of patriarchy is a further hierarchy among women.

Although few women have complete access to power within Canadian society, some women face more barriers than others. For example, the relatively stronger social position of a well-educated, white, affluent daughter or mother may not protect her from male violence but it will certainly increase her chances of being believed if she seeks help. A police officer may be more likely to urge her to press charges if he believes that, as the victim, she will make an articulate, credible witness in court. On the flip side, an immigrant domestic worker who speaks little English or French is less likely to be believed by police or judges. This is not an assumption; unfortunately, this is a reality.

For the purposes of discussion in the Final Report we grouped the specific populations as follows: older women, women living in poverty including women with low literacy skills, women with disabilities, rural women, lesbians, women of official language minorities, women of colour, young women and immigrant and refugee women and domestic workers.

In addition to chapters on each of these populations, there are quite extensive examinations of the situation of Inuit and Aboriginal women. The unique and difficult circumstances of these women can be traced back to the time of initial European contact. Economic development, revitalization of indigeonous cultures, use of

traditional healing methods and rapid movement toward self-government are all parts of a multi-faceted strategy which must be adopted if the continuing tragedy of violence in Aboriginal communities is to be curtailed.

The grouping of certain categories of women together does not suggest that they are homogenous, with exactly the same characteristics, problems and needs, but they do share certain barriers to equality and particular vulnerabilities to violence. Although the focus of this part of the Final Report is on violence and its relationship to individual populations, the discussion is relevant to all women.

Again, the voices of those who have experienced or witnessed the violence are most eloquent.

The survivor was married for 50 years to a verbally abusive man who expressed controlling behaviour toward the family and had sole control of the finances. He attempted to hit her on many occasions, and did strike her when she was older. The husband developed dementia in his later years, and all his negative characteristics came to the fore. He couldn't control his temper. On one occasion, he pushed her to the floor, resulting in permanent injury to a weak hip. She now has a pin in her hip and arthritis. He would not help her get up and denied pushing her. He would also deny his verbal abuse .... The husband went away on business trips and left no money behind .... She never knew where she stood with him; he could adopt a "pleasing attitude" so the abuse was not obvious to others. He treated his son and daughter differently: his son could do no wrong, his daughter no right. There is intense pressure on women to give care. "You resent it, but you do it ...." The attitude professionals took to the survivor's situation was, "How could she abandon him, when she's put up with it for so long?"

I'm a small-town girl who married someone and was with him for 11 years. I left him three times. You're fighting at every step of the way. I have nothing good to say about the legal system. Nothing is explained to you, nothing is shown to you, nothing is given to you at all. I don't like the term "domestic violence" because it takes away from exactly what happens to you. It's assault. I left with three children, a suitcase, $20 and a box of Tide. It took a long time to get financial support. The process you have to go through is humiliating: welfare, the legal system.

♀ ♀ ♀

A deaf woman was raped and the judge asked her why she didn't say no. The judge let the rapist off because he said he couldn't understand her testimony ....

♀ ♀ ♀

I hope that the hell is over. I live in a rural area with my two young children. The Ontario Provincial Police have told me that the fastest they can get to my house in an emergency is one hour. Between 2 a.m. and 6 a.m. there is no one available at all.

♀ ♀ ♀

Two women I know who were partners taught riding at the same riding school. They came out to their truck one day and found the word "lesbians" spray-painted on it in large letters. Soon after, one of the woman was brought before a meeting of the entire board of directors and publicly accused of being a lesbian. She was then fired. The second woman was fired shortly thereafter.

♀ ♀ ♀

A Francophone woman in a crisis situation who needs immediate help will use the language spoken by "everybody" so as to be sure of being understood. It takes all the courage she has to seek help. She has no energy left to start debating language issues.

♀ ♀ ♀

Racism has the same effects among Black people — loss of dignity, respect, control, inability to protect self and family, and the loss of respect of the Black community for

their family — as does wife battering to family members. Black women have already been burdened, humiliated and ravaged by those factors from birth.

♀ ♀ ♀

Women experience sexual harassment everywhere. Guys in cars honk at you, bosses, colleagues, fellow students, professors ... there's sexist jokes, comments, movies, commercials. It's everywhere and people seem to think it's just a normal part of the way things work.

♀ ♀ ♀

I remember the first time I think something was funny was one night, I was sleeping and I feel someone in my clothing, feeling up my private parts. This happened after I was here for a month. I jumped up because I was frighten and when I look it was him — the man I was working for. He hold my mouth and tell me to be quiet. He smell of alcohol and I did not know where his wife was, but it was late at night. He kept pushing his finger down in my private parts and blowing hard. When I told him it hurt he asked me if I didn't birth to one baby already. He tried to push me down on the bed but I wouldn't let him. After he finished, he jumped off me, spit on the floor, and tell me if I tell his wife or anybody he would send me back to — or that I go to jail. I was really frightened. I really believed that I could get locked up. For what, I don't know, it happened seven or eight times. I was scared to tell anybody, further I didn't know where to turn to. I didn't know anybody here.

♀ ♀ ♀

The fact is that it [immigration law] is giving an extreme weight to the sponsoring partner in the immigration process, and this [means that], when violence against the woman happens she is doubly punished. My three friends were very clear that the power gap between them and their husbands made them stay in their relationships. They were helpless, fearing an extra humiliation: to go back to their country when there was little left there.

Because of our [Inuit] culture, we require different solutions to our problems. Because of our isolation and the smallness of our population, we require local and culturally appropriate remedies. Women need to be recognized as one of the most important pillars of our communities.

♀♀♀

There were many abuses of Inuit women by qallunaat [non-Inuit]; sometimes they would get jealous and beat women up. I used to hear about qallunaat going after Inuit wives. I once heard that people were starving at one place and so a wife had sex with the qallunaat there in exchange for tea and sugar .... I have heard about Inuit selling their wives. They didn't want to at first, but the qallunaat traded things like bullets and tobacco for sex. The Inuit got paid for sharing their wives .... That's how it began.

♀♀♀

Our traditional [Inuit] values have broken down; [they are] still there, but weak. We are trying to take on the values of the dominant culture. Children were sent to boarding schools because our parents were afraid they would lose the family allowance if they refused to send us. Organized religion was shoved down our throats .... I remember being in school and being slapped if I spoke my own language. That was a heavy situation. No one else in the world would allow themselves to be treated like that .... The white man came along and said that he knew who made the sun that shines down on us. I am not picking on the culture that came from across the water, but a genocide happened. [It] needs to be recognized that it is a violent past — tuberculosis, smallpox, genocide.

♀♀♀

Overcrowded housing doesn't by itself cause spousal assault, but no one can deny the family pressure that builds up over time as a result of overcrowding and lack of privacy is a [contributing factor] of spouse assault.

Overcrowded housing is not by itself the reason why so few young Inuit are graduating from high school, but the pressures of overcrowding, the lack of quiet places to study, etc. surely don't help. Overcrowding housing did not by itself cause the TB outbreaks in Repulse Bay and Rae-Edzo, or the E.Coli 0157 outbreak in Arviat that claimed several lives last year, but the overcrowded and run-down housing definitely contributed to their spread.

Before the arrival of the European civilization, women were powerful. Since then, the western [non-Native] civilization has come and told men that they must take control. From here on in, we must, as women, reopen the eyes of our men, by claiming our positions as leaders and healers.

♀♀♀

Gang rapes happen, on and off reserve, white men and Aboriginal men, young women and old women. A young girl was at a party, her stepfather and her uncle raped her in front of a friend and some young boys. They stuffed her mouth with pills to try and kill her to prevent her from telling. The friend and the young boys tried to stop it from happening. When the friend told the community social services worker what had happened, the community told the girl it was her fault that she got raped because she went to the party. She pressed charges and the judge asked her if she wanted to continue. The stepfather killed himself, and then it came out that there was incest all through the family over generations.

♀♀♀

My mother lost her cultural ways and never went back to the reserve ... I was never taught to feel proud of my heritage .... There is a perception that 'white reality' is the absolute reality, and this is part of the balance of power .... Aboriginal cultures need to be revitalized, and women elders need to come out and be recognized for the strong leaders they are.

EXPERIENCING VIOLENCE ~ INSTITUTIONS

A central part of our mandate has been to develop a National Action Plan to address the issue of violence against women. Any plan that targets such a complex and multi-dimensional subject must have, as its cornerstone, the goal of social change. The prerequisites for such change are knowledge and understanding of the issue; a detailed strategy for effecting change; a broad-based commitment to implementing that strategy; and a mechanism for periodically reviewing the progress of implementation. In Part Four of the Final Report, Experiencing Violence – Institutions, we elaborate on the weaknesses and shortcomings of significant social institutions in responding to the safety and security needs of women in Canada. This critique forms the basis, ultimately, for our National Action Plan. The major issues identified for each institution are summarized in the Key Problems section of each of the sector plans which appear in the National Action Plan.

In the first part of our report, we spoke about the need to develop a "way of thinking" about violence against women that places individual acts of violence in a larger sociological context. Such an approach is essential for understanding the breadth, depth and persistence of violence against women, not only today but throughout history.

We emphasized the link between some of the conditions that women face in Canada today and the violence they face. These conditions are the outcome of the current social, economic, political and cultural context which can only be changed by altering social institutions. These changes, we argue, will provide the groundwork for a society that is safe for women.

In Part Four of our report, we identify and examine those social institutions that are the most salient to our understanding and to changing current patterns of gender, race and class inequality. These institutions impinge on women's lives on a daily basis. The legal system,

the media, the health care system, the workplace, various service delivery areas, the education system and other key government sectors figure prominently in women's experiences of violence. Any analysis of these is strengthened by the voices and experiences of the survivors of violence: their lives provide the filter for our framework and recommendations. It is from these women, along with a multitude of people working in all aspects of this issue, that we have taken our cue.

Institutions must not be perceived as neutral settings that treat and are experienced by everyone in a similar fashion. Women and men experience life differently because of their gender; and, for some women the gender difference is compounded by race, class, ability level, age and sexual orientation. There is a bias in which social institutions, settings or programs operate to the advantage of one gender, race or class and to the disadvantage of others.

Tolerance of violence against women is unquestionably present in the social institutions we examined. In the health care system, many professionals remain indifferent to the continuation of the violence. Institutional personnel who may not behave violently themselves witness violent acts committed against women clients and make little or no effort to stop it. Indeed they may simply turn a blind eye to it. The atmosphere within many schools whether at the primary, secondary or university level is hostile to young women.

The legal system remains self-serving, perpetuating ineffective and inadequate laws, policies, practices — and indeed, practitioners — which only serve to continue the denial of violence against women. The rights of the accused who is almost invariably a male in cases of violence are protected in accordance with long-standing traditions in our legal systems; the rights of the victim who is usually female to equal protection of the law and to security of the person is secondary. And as her safety interests are compromised, so too are those of all women. In the military, women are subjected to sexist behaviour, language and treatment that undermine their personal power and jeopardize their career aspirations. In the workplace, the absence of sexual and gender harassment policies, and the protracted nature of pursuing charges, often mean that women have to tolerate a hostile, dangerous and poisoned work atmosphere or lose their jobs.

Even when attempts have been made to address the scope and dimension of violence against women, these attempts, taken together, have been partial, incomplete and ill-conceived.

The voices of women recounting their experiences with social or health services, with the legal system, in the workplace in the military, in the education system, the media and in religious institutions make a powerful case for the radical change and realignment of priorities proposed in our National Action Plan.

We should not have to tear down other programs to get money, and we should not have to run bingos to run services.

♀ ♀ ♀

There is a lack of support for survivors to heal. When I started out two and a half years ago there were women who dealt with sexual abuse but only after three or four disclosures. We need a place they feel safe enough to come to in the first place.

♀ ♀ ♀

Social welfare agencies are terribly abusive to women in need. They treat us like second-class citizens. Social workers can be abusive, disrespectful, dangerous.

♀ ♀ ♀

I moved into the city because of the accident, because my family did not know how to take care of me. Even the nurses down there don't know how to work with people with disabilities, so I had to come to the city even though I didn't want to.

People don't believe that ritual abuse happens ... professionals do not get the training required ... and so they give inappropriate counselling or treatment.

♀ ♀ ♀

Without accompanying jail time, treatment for offenders is a token gesture and an ineffective remedy for a serious crime. Instead of causing men to confront their violence, it allows them to reinforce the societal bias that their actions do not constitute a crime.

♀ ♀ ♀

The professors and male students [at medical school] would make jokes. "It is just a joke," they would say, but I would look around and none of the women were laughing.

♀ ♀ ♀

I worked in a psychiatric facility in another province. I saw punishment and ridicule of patients for being sick. I even saw physical violence .... We had a union rule which was too weak — it stated that a worker had to be caught physically abusing a patient three times before firing was permissible.

♀ ♀ ♀

Officers are assigned to investigate sexual assault complaints when they are clearly uncomfortable dealing with the subject. Investigators are inadequately trained.

♀ ♀ ♀

Every police department [must] have a clearly defined and publicized accountability process, explain why charges are not laid, allow for a review of these cases.

♀ ♀ ♀

The rights of the victim are trampled to protect those of the defendant. The job of the prosecutor is not to defend the victim, but rather to protect the interests of the state. On the day of trial, the Crown prosecutor did not even introduce himself to her.

Women who have been through the court process believed there had been very little accountability from the system for its treatment of women. Almost none felt they had been dealt with fairly.

♀♀♀

I was forced into legal aid mediation from 9 a.m. to 1 a.m. and forced into an agreement mandated by the director of legal aid. I was not allowed to take a break. The agreement was not in my interest or my son's interest. I was threatened that my legal aid would be taken away. There are tons of loopholes that my husband is using. My husband is using the court system to abuse me. He is raping me financially, physically, sexually.

♀♀♀

Pornography is the most graphic representation of the attitude toward women which makes rape, wife battering, incest, sexual harassment and women's economic inequality, among other things, possible.

♀♀♀

Violence is far less likely between equals ... therefore, equality and respect of all people is a crucial concept which must be realized ... women have not yet achieved equality and this must be redressed. Otherwise our equality is not guaranteed.

♀♀♀

[I] was assigned to [a] suicidal patient who was hallucinating; in the course of five minutes the course of my life was changed. I felt a crunch of my face. I suffered a serious assault that ended my career as a nurse. Although the assault was a crime, I was discouraged [from] laying charges by the administration. The violence I suffered was not acknowledged ....

It's too easy for society to excuse men by saying that's just how they are. For example, when someone reported sexual harassment, the boss just said, "well, that's just how men are," and that's a typical reaction when women complain, then there is no discipline taken at all against the men.

♀♀♀

There I was with two children and three suitcases representing 20 years of marriage — no home, and still hundreds of miles from family, no support, no medical coverage .... My self-esteem was non-existent and my self-confidence shattered. I did not deserve to be treated like landfill refuse and neither did my children. The Department of National Defence stood by my husband in the days following and allowed him to deny support for his family, forcing us to go on welfare. This proud soldier even denied food for his own children and still the military refused to help. Finally after a few weeks in slow legal processes, a garnishment was enacted and stopped us from becoming street people.

♀♀♀

I've seen a lot of girls "gotten" in the hallway — pushed up against the wall and called bitch, slut, ... [and they] have to deal with come-ons.

♀♀♀

There is concern with safety issues around schools. Young women's safety is very different than that of young men's. Girls are often "rated" as they walk down halls. Guys do this secretly ... sometimes loudly, as you walk by.

♀♀♀

Schools often don't recognize that little girls (3, 4, 5 years old) are facing sexism, violence, etc. from the boys; it is often not recognized or acknowledged until girls reach puberty.

♀♀♀

The educational material reinforces stereo-types. Children think it's the norm, like math-ematics discourages girls from going into sci-ences ... one of our teachers told his students that maths and sciences were for boys. This incident was reported and nothing was done about it. Students think the teacher has got to be right, teachers know all, that's the danger.

♀ ♀ ♀

The schools could include [the topic of] date rape for example in a human relations course for both sexes — when they do it now, it's for the girls only; the guys need to take these courses too.

♀ ♀ ♀

At a high school located in a middle-class neighbourhood, a women's issues group put up a number of posters explaining the mean-ing of feminism ... what feminism is and isn't, what lesbians are .... The posters were torn down or had the words "Nazi" and "bitches" written all over them .... The group was told that by putting up the posters they were asking for trouble ....

♀ ♀ ♀

With some exceptions, media images of women continue to be stereotypical, sexist and demeaning. Women of colour, lesbians, women as experts and in positions of authority are still rare.

♀ ♀ ♀

The daily newspaper is a central aspect of any society. The casual inclusion of women as a commodity to be taken with morning coffee and last night's baseball scores is clearly an "everyday feature of Canadian life" that promotes male dominance and female subordination.

At present the Canadian government delivers a double message about violence against women by, on the one hand, funding emergency services and treatment programs for victims, and on the other, refusing to take action at a structural level to outlaw the production and distribution of material that perpetuates the subordination of women.

ENDNOTES

1   United Nations, *Declaration on the Elimination of Violence Against Women*, p. 6. The UN Commission on the Status of Women approved the draft in March 1993. The draft will go forward to the General Assembly in the fall of 1993. (Canada initiated the declaration.)

2   *Ibid.*

3   G. Larouche, *Agir contre la violence* (Montreal: Éditions La pleine lune, 1987), p. 32.

4   Dominique Bilodeau "L'approche féministe en maison d'hébergement : quand la pratique enrichit la théorie," *Nouvelles pratiques sociales*, Vol. 3, No. 2, (1990): 48

5   Barbara Hart, *Safety For Women: Monitoring Batterers' Programs* (Harrisburg: Pennsylvania Coalition Against Domestic Violence, 1988), p. 18.

6   Sub-Committee on the Status of Women, *The War Against Women: Report of the Standing Committee on Health and Welfare, Social Affairs, Seniors and the Status of Women* (Ottawa: House of Commons, June 1991).

7   Lori Haskell and Melanie Randall, *The Women's Safety Project: Summary of Key Statistical Findings* (Ottawa: Canadian Panel on Violence Against Women, 1993). The Canadian Panel on Violence Against Women has published the *Summary of Key Statistical Findings* resulting from the work of the Women's Safety Project as an appendix to this report. Unless otherwise indicated, all references to the Women's Safety Project in the body of the report can be found in detail in Appendix A.

8   Maclean's-CTV, "Anxieties Over Violence," *Maclean's*, Vol. 105, No. 01 (January 4, 1993), p. 25.

9   L. Chénard, H. Cadrin and J. Loiselle, *État de santé des femmes et des enfants victimes de violence conjugale* (Rimouski, Que.: Département de santé communautaire, Centre hospitalier régional de Rimouski, Octobre, 1990), p. 71.

10   *Ibid.*

11   *Ibid.,* p. 41.

12   Andrée Côté, *La rage au coeur : rapport de recherche sur le traitement judiciaire de l'homicide conjugal au Québec* (Baie Comeau, Que.: Regroupement des femmes de la Côte-Nord, 1991), p. 139.

13   Jacqueline Dupuis, "L'urgence, le premier contact," *Nursing Québec*, Vol. 5, No. 5 (1985): 24.

14   J. Groeneveld and M. Shain, *Drug Abuse Among Victims of Physical and Sexual Abuse: A Preliminary Report* (Toronto: Addiction Research Foundation, 1989), p. 8.

15   Louise Vandelac, Diane Bélisle, Anne Gauthier and Yolande Pinard, *Du travail et de l'amour* (Montreal Saint-Martin, 1986), *passim.*

16   United Nations Development Program, *Human Development Report 1992*, (New York: Oxford University Press, 1993).

17   Statistics Canada, "Earnings of Men and Women", in *The Daily*, January 14th, 1993, p.3.

18   Abdul Rashid, "Seven Decades of Wage Changes", in *Perspectives on Labour and Income*, Volume 5, No. 2, Summer 1993, pp. 13 & 18.

19   Statistics Canada, "1991 Census: Highlights", in *The Daily*, April 13th, 1993, p.1.

20   *Ibid*, p.1

21   *Ibid*, p.3

22   Statistics Canada, "Women in Academia — A Growing Minority", in *The Daily*, March 11th, 1993, p.3.

23   Nancy Zukewich Graham, "Women in the Workplace", in *Canadian Social Trends*, No. 28, Spring 1993, p.6.

24   *Ibid*, p.6.

25   Canada Health Monitor, "Highlights Report Survey # 6", January 1992, Price Waterhouse and Earl Berger, Toronto 1992, p.3.

26   Statistics Canada, Women in Canada — A Statistical Report, Minister of Supply and Services, Ottawa, 1990, p.27.

27   *Ibid*, pp. 108-109.

28   Canadian Centre for Justice Statistics, "Correctional Expenditures and Personnel in Canada", in *Juristat*, Vol. 12, No. 22, November 30th, 1992, p.1, and, Statistics Canada, *Adult Correctional Services in Canada — 1991-92*, Ottawa 1992.

29   Statistics Canada, *Women in Canada — A Statistical Report, op.cit.*, p.147.

30   National Action Committee on the Status of Women, "Review of the Situation of Women in Canada - 1992", Toronto, May 1992, p.12.

31   G. Lerner, *The Creation of Patriarchy* (New York: Oxford University Press, 1986), p. 239.

32   Ginette Larouche, *Agir contre la violence* (Montreal: Editions La Pleine lune, 1987), p. 35.

33   Micheline de Sève, *Pour un féminisme libertaire* (Saint-Laurent: Boréal Express, 1985), p. 118.

34   Department of Justice Canada, Research Section, *Sexual Assault Legislation in Canada: An Evaluation: Overview (Report No. 5)* (Ottawa, 1990), pp. 13-14.

35   Maria Crawford and Rosemary Gartner, *Woman Killing, Intimate Femicide in Ontario 1974-1990* (Toronto: The Women We Honour Action Committee, 1992), p. 52.

36   Statistics Canada, *The Daily,* March 2, 1993, p. 10.

37   Nancy Adamson, Linda Briskin and Margaret McPhail, *Feminist Organizing for Change: The Contemporary Women's Movement in Canada* (Toronto: Oxford University Press, 1988), p. 110.

38   C. Allen and J. Persad, "Fighting Racism and Sexism Together," as cited in N.L. Adamson et al., *ibid.*, p. 106.

39   Maria Crawford and Rosemary Gartner, *Woman Killing: Intimate Femicide in Ontario 1974-1990* (Toronto: Women We Honour Action Committee), p. 27.

PART
TWO

THE NATIONAL
ACTION PLAN

THE NATIONAL ACTION PLAN

Introduction

This section of the report addresses the solutions to the problem of violence against women. The Panel believes that inequality increases women's vulnerability to violence and limits their choices in all aspects of their lives. In turn, women cannot achieve full equality while they are subjected to violence in their daily lives. The Panel is therefore committed to two goals: the achievement of women's equality and the elimination of violence against women. The National Action Plan (NAP) identifies concrete steps twoard the achievement of both goals. The proposed actions are neither simple nor easy to implement. They demand a sustained and co-ordinated response. They demand a new set of priorities and a new way of looking at the world. They also demand recognition of the differences among women and the diverse approaches required to address the concerns of all women.

The National Action Plan begins by calling on our goverments to fulfil their international commitments with respect to women's equality. When women have achieved legal, economic, social and political equality they will be able to make choices in their lives which truly reflect their interests. They will no longer have to suffer violence out of fear, poverty, shame or powerlessness. The Equality Action Plan deals with those aspects of formal equality that the Panel believes have the greatest bearing on the vulnerability of women to violence.

- Equality rights

- Equal access to the legal system

- Political and public service participation

- Mechanisms for women

- Women and the economy

- The Family

- Women and the tax/transfer system

The National Action Plan introduces the concept of zero tolerance and a policy framework for its implementation. Zero tolerance means that no level of violence is acceptable, and women's safety and equality are priorities. All organizations and institutions are strongly encouraged to review their programs, practices and products in light of the Zero Tolerance Policy which includes:

- an accountability framework;

- implementation steps; and

- a zero tolerance model for organizations and institutions to follow.

The policy is applied to key sectors in society — services (health and social), legal, workplace, military, education, media, religious institutions and the federal government — to illustrate the nature and magnitude of the changes required to ensure safety and equality for women in Canada.

Health and social services and the legal/justice system are crucial to women since these sectors often offer first response when violence happens. Women look to these sectors for protection, redress and healing.

The education system, the media and religious institutions shape attitudes and behaviours, and have a critical role to play in advancing equality and ending violence. The workplace, a site of much violence against women, is key to women gaining economic independence and thereby reducing their vulnerability to violence.

The military is dominated by men and male values. Newly admitted as workers in a full range of occupations, women face discrimination, harassment and violence. Spouses of military men are also deeply affected by military policy and culture.

Governments have a major role in protecting women's rights, promoting equality and providing leadership to the application of the Zero Tolerance Policy.

Application of the Zero Tolerance Policy in these eight sectors will provide a foundation for zero tolerance at every level in Canada. It is not just up to governments, institutions and organizations to ensure equality and safety for women: individuals and communities also have a role to play. Therefore, in the Action Plan for Individuals, we have provided examples of actions which individuals can take as intimate partners, parents, children, friends, co-workers and community members.

We conclude by proposing accountabilty and monitoring mechanisms to ensure that the National Action Plan is fully reviewed and responded to. The Zero Tolerance Policy underscores the importance of accountability at all levels and in all sectors. It is critical that the federal government, which must take the lead in implementing the National Action Plan through its various departments, be closely monitored to assess the adequacy of its activities both at the individual departmental level and collectively in accordance with a zero tolerance approach to violence against women.

*   *Although all of the actions enumerated in the National Action Plan are applicable to all women in Canada, actions which apply uniquely to Aboriginal and/or Inuit women are noted by use of the following symbols:*

 Aboriginal   *Inuit*

SECTION 1

EQUALITY ACTION PLAN

Introduction

Equality has been defined as,

> ... both a goal and a means whereby
> individuals are accorded equal treatment
> under the law and equal opportunities to
> enjoy their rights and to develop their
> potential talents and skills so that they can
> participate in national political, economic,
> social and cultural development and can
> benefit from its results. For women in
> particular, equality means the realization of
> rights that have been denied as a result of
> cultural, institutional, behavioural and
> attitudinal discrimination. [1]

Canada already has a strong, stated commitment to
gender equality and a legacy of statutory measures
aimed at achieving equality. The *Canadian Charter of
Rights and Freedoms*, employment equity and human
rights legislation at the federal, provincial and territorial levels are all manifestations of our commitment to equality. However, while Canadian law provides, in broad terms, for equality and non-
discrimination, true gender equality in which women
participate equally in all facets of society is not the
day-to-day reality. Statistical profiles of women in
Canada consistently describe the specific economic,
political, social or cultural forms women's inequality
can take. The experiences of Canadian girls and
women reflect these statistical measures every day.

In addition to its domestic measures, Canada has
made clear and unequivocal international commitments to achieving equality for women by signing a
number of international conventions and declara-
tions. These include the Universal Declaration of
Human Rights, [2] the United Nations Convention on
the Elimination of All Forms of Discrimination against
Women, [3] including General recommendation
No. 19 [4] which specifically addresses the issue of
violence against women, and the adoption in 1985 of
the Nairobi Forward-looking Strategies for the
Advancement of Women.

We believe that concrete, practical fulfilment of
these commitments along with significant change in
key areas of women's lives would make a critical
difference in achieving women's equality in our
society, thereby reducing women's vulnerability to
violence.

While women face systemic barriers and inequality
in all sectors of society, we have chosen to focus on
the following fundamental dimensions of women's
lives: formal legal equality, equal access to the legal
system, political and public service participation,
national mechanisms to promote women's equality,
participation in the economy, the family and the role
of women within it, and the tax system.

Although we have not been able to deal with all the
subjects that would comprise a comprehensive
equality agenda, we want to underscore that full
equality will only be achieved when biases and
discrimination no longer exist in any aspect of
women's lives.

Two underlying principles guided us in our selection
of recommendations. First, there is the need to
enhance women's economic independence — the
lack of which is inherently tied to women's
experience of violence and which limits their options
once violence has occurred. This can best be
achieved through measures such as equal access to
work opportunities, fair compensation for work
performed, the provision of support at key
transition points in the lives of women and sufficient
income in retirement. Second, women must be
recognized and treated as autonomous beings,
distinct from their familial relationships and from
their male partners in particular.

Unless otherwise specified, our recommendations are directed to the federal level of government. This is not to downplay the role that provincial and municipal governments, organizations, communities and individuals must play in achieving equality for women but rather to recognize the responsibility of the federal government to demonstrate leadership in the fulfilment of Canada's national and international commitments. We expect action to begin immediately. This is in keeping with Canada's commitment to the implementation of the Nairobi Forward-looking Strategies which aim at achieving equality for women by the year 2000.

Equality requires that no adverse distinctions be made on the basis of race, class, sexual orientation, linguistic, immigrant or visible minority status, age or ability. When we talk about the achievement of equality, we mean equality for all women. We recognize, however, that equality does not necessarily mean treating all women the same. There may need to be differential treatment for some women in order for all women to realize their full potential. In many cases, we have identified changes which must be made to our laws, to political and governmental practices, to our economy and culture to ensure the full participation of specific groups of women.

The recommendations are not in any order of priority. They are all important and in most cases, complementary.

I EQUALITY RIGHTS

In Canada, equality rights are fundamentally enshrined in the *Canadian Charter of Rights and Freedoms* and in federal, provincial and territorial human rights legislation.

Key Problems

*   The laws which specifically address equality do not refer expressly to certain women (for example, lesbians) nor do they offer adequate protection against discrimination (for example, in the case of Aboriginal people).

*   Human rights legislation is insufficient to help women achieve equality. There are major limitations with respect to the scope, application, remedies and enforcement of the legislation, and its individual, complaints-based processes.

*   The lives of certain Aboriginal women are governed by the *Indian Act*, which means that in some cases their equality rights are compromised.

*   Women refugees often face gender bias before coming to Canada and on their arrival in Canada. Their experiences are not adequately recognized by our laws.

Canada's Commitment:

To ensure a legal basis for the equal rights of women. [5]

Fulfilling Canada's commitment includes:

E.1 **Adding sexual orientation as one of the prohibited grounds of discrimination in the *Canadian Human Rights Act* and to provincial and territorial human rights legislation where it does not presently exist, without limitation with respect to the definition of family or marital status.**

E.2 **Ensuring that human rights legislation has the power to address systemic discrimination, as well as individual, complaint-driven cases of discrimination.**

E.3 **Guaranteeing that Aboriginal women are recognized and protected in the human rights legislation which applies in all provinces and territories regardless of treaty rights.**

E.4 **Eliminating the discrimination among different categories of Aboriginal women and their children in the *Indian Act*.**

E.5 **Realizing Aboriginal, including Métis, aspirations for self-government, guaranteeing the direct participation of Aboriginal women and protecting their rights under the *Canadian Charter of Rights and Freedoms* in the negotiation of any agreements, treaties or land claim settlements.**

E.6 **Changing, through legislation, the grounds for granting refugee status to recognize persecution on the basis of gender explicitly.**

II EQUAL ACCESS TO THE LEGAL SYSTEM

Women's lives are governed by the general laws of Canadian society which are based on British Common Law and the French Civil Code. These laws embody the values, customs and traditions of societies which have been dominated and largely shaped by European males. As such, they do not reflect the unique experiences and circumstances of women, nor do they take into account the realities of different groups of women such as Aboriginal women, Inuit women, women of colour, immigrant women, refugee women, young women, older women, women with disabilities and lesbians.

The laws and the manner in which they are interpreted and applied have a direct bearing on the choices and experiences of women who are victims of violence.

Key Problems

- Laws which appear to be gender neutral may have a differential and adverse impact on women.

- Not all women have equal access to the legal system. Women are often unaware of their rights due to the absence of appropriate and accessible information. Many lack the resources, particularly financial, to exercise their rights.

- Not all women are treated equally before the law. Women frequently face overt discrimination by those responsible for enforcing the law. If they are members of Aboriginal, Inuit or ethnic communities, or if they are immigrant or refugee women, they may encounter racist and ethnocentric attitudes in addition to the discrimination they face on the basis of gender. Lesbians and women with disabilities may also have to contend with heterosexist and stereotypical images of what constitutes a "normal" woman.

- For certain women — members of Aboriginal, Inuit, immigrant, refugee and minority language groups — language barriers restrict access to the justice system. Others, namely Aboriginal and Inuit women and women living in rural or isolated areas, encounter difficulties due to the absence of services. For women with disabilities or low literacy skills, the lack of services in alternative forms creates a barrier.

- Unlike criminal law, there are no national standards for the provision of legal aid in civil law cases. This can severely limit women's opportunities for redress or settlement, particularly in family law actions.

- Current Aboriginal justice system projects do not respond to the specific needs and concerns of Aboriginal women.

Canada's Commitment:

To establish legislative and administrative mechanisms to ensure that individual women and women as a group may, without obstruction or cost to themselves, obtain redress for both discriminatory actions and systemic discrimination.

Fulfilling Canada's commitment includes:

E.7   **Reinstating and expanding the Court Challenges Program,[6] extending its application to provincial and territorial laws, and providing full and adequate funding for its application by the respective level of government.**

E.8   **Strengthening human rights legislation in consultation with equality-seeking groups, and adequately financing the Canadian Human Rights Commission and its provincial and territorial counterparts to pursue women's equality, investigate systemic discrimination and provide redress, and more efficiently and effectively resolve individual cases of discrimination.**

Canada's Commitment:

To investigate the problems associated with the relationship between the law, and the role, status and material circumstances of women.

Fulfilling Canada's commitment includes:

E.9   **Funding equality-seeking groups to build upon the gender equality work of the Canadian Bar Association and law societies across Canada by reviewing all legislation and common law principles to determine if they have a differential or negative impact on women, or particular groups of women, and amending them accordingly.**

E.10   **Establishing national standards and financing for the provision of legal aid for family law cases.**

E.11   **Working with provincial and territorial governments to implement mandatory gender and race sensitivity training for all law students, lawyers, judges and para-legal personnel.**

E.12   **Guaranteeing the equal participation of Aboriginal and Inuit women in the design and implementation of Aboriginal and Inuit justice systems.**

III POLITICAL AND PUBLIC SERVICE PARTICIPATION

In general, women are under-represented in Canada's political institutions and the public service. As a result, laws, policies and programs do not reflect women's priorities, meet their needs or respond to their concerns. For example, there is insufficient funding for programs to promote equality or eliminate violence; the health care system does not respond adequately to female victims of violence and women's health issues in general; and economic policies do not recognize women's unpaid contributions, their work patterns or their poverty.

Key Problems

In Politics

- The dominant ethic in politics is neither receptive nor particularly attractive to women.

- Women, especially Aboriginal women, women of colour and women with disabilities, are under-represented in all political parties and in elected offices in Canada.

- Women are overrepresented in the volunteer ranks of political parties, but are often employed in menial tasks and are under-represented in decision-making positions.

- There are financial barriers to women's political participation at all levels.

- Women frequently face harassment and denigration when participating in politics.

- Aboriginal leaders in local, regional and national governments are not accountable to Aboriginal women and, therefore, do not adequately uphold their rights nor advance their issues.

In the Public Service

- Despite measures to rectify historical imbalances, women are under-represented at the higher levels of decision making in the public service. [7]

- The *Employment Equity Act* does not extend to Parliament, the federal public service or federal agencies, boards and commissions. [8] Treasury Board's Employment Equity Policy has only led to modest progress in the representation, recruitment, promotion and retention of target group members. [9]

Canada's Commitment:

To ensure equality of participation by women at all levels of government, to encourage women to exercise their political rights and to provide equal access to the ranks of political parties and other organizations.

Fulfilling Canada's commitment includes:

E.13 Implementing the recommendations regarding the full participation of women in the political process contained in the report of the Royal Commission on Electoral Reform and Party Financing, *Reforming Electoral Democracy*. [10] Similar recommendations should be extended to provincial and municipal politics.

E.14 Encouraging Aboriginal and Inuit women to assume leadership roles in all levels of government.

E.15 Developing and implementing a policy against harassment — including harassment on the basis of sex, race, religion, ethnic origin, age and sexual orientation or level of ability — for members of Parliament, their staff and federal political parties.

E.16   Implementing the recommendations contained in the report of the Task Force on Barriers to Women in the Public Service, *Beneath the Veneer*.

E.17   Extending the application of the *Employment Equity Act* to Parliament, the federal public service and all federal agencies, boards and commissions. Furthermore, ensuring that all federal political parties report to Parliament, on an annual basis, on the composition of their staff and the staff of members of Parliament.

IV MECHANISMS FOR WOMEN

Canada has established a variety of mechanisms to promote equality for women. At the federal level these include the Minister Responsible for the Status of Women and her department, Status of Women Canada (SWC), the Canadian Advisory Council on the Status of Women (CACSW), women's bureaus and programs or advisors in a variety of departments. In addition, the Women's Program of the Secretary of State provides funding to assist national, regional and local groups to pursue equality for women through a variety of activities.

These mechanisms, and in particular women's groups, have been essential in raising public awareness, taking action on issues of concern to women including violence against women, and in lobbying to put women's issues on the political agenda.

Key Problems

•   No federal government department has the statutory authority to develop, oversee and co-ordinate the implementation of the government's agenda for women and to ensure that gender equality is promoted and achieved through all federal policies, programs and legislation.

•   Policies, programs and legislative proposals are often developed without the involvement of the federal mechanisms for women. When these mechanisms are consulted, it is frequently after policy directions have been set.

•   Within departments, women's bureaus or advisors are frequently bypassed, sidelined or ignored in the development of legislation, policies or programs.

•   The diversity of Canadian women is not adequately reflected in the composition or substantive work of many government mechanisms for women.

•   The contributions of non-governmental organizations in articulating women's views, monitoring and evaluating government products and advocating for change, are not adequately recognized, nor are such organizations adequately funded, consulted or involved in legislation, policy and program development.

Canada's Commitment:

To strengthen national mechanisms for monitoring and improving the status of women at all levels in the government and ensure adequate resources, commitment and authority to advise on the impact on women of all government policies, programs and legislation; to disseminate information to women regarding their rights and entitlements; and to cooperate with other government agencies and non-governmental organizations.

Fulfilling Canada's commitment includes:

E.18   Enacting a "Status of Women Act" to identify the specific obligations and responsibilities of the federal government to ensure that the rights to equality and safety of all Canadian women are supported and advanced.

The Act would:

- **Designate the Minister Responsible for the Status of Women as a senior minister with the power and authority to enforce the Act, including the development and implementation of a multi-year plan with clear objectives and target dates aimed at achieving gender equality and implementing a policy of zero tolerance.**

- **Provide the Minister with the authority to participate, with the support of the Status of Women ministry, in the development and final review of all federal government policies, programs and legislative proposals for their impact on all women and to propose amendments as required.**

- **Enhance the capacity of the Status of Women ministry to support the Minister through the provision of adequate resources for consultation,** research, policy development and analysis, and to monitor the government's progress on equality and women's safety.

- **Develop a framework for equality and safety to guide departments in their policy analysis, program development and legislative drafting to increase sensitivity to gender and the differences among women as a result of age, ability, race, colour, sexual orientation or other characteristics.**

- **Ensure the full participation of national groups seeking equality for women in the implementation of the Act, through the creation of a permanent Advisory Board. Among its members, the Board would include Aboriginal and Inuit women, women of colour, immigrants, lesbians and women with disabilities. Board members would provide policy advice and guidance to the Status of Women ministry, particularly with respect to the government's multi-year gender-equality plan and the development of the equality and safety framework. The exact membership, role and responsibilities of the Advisory Board would be determined in consultation with relevant groups.**

- **Make the government accountable for its progress on women's equality and safety by requiring the Minister to report to Parliament, on an annual basis, on the gender impact and consequences of government policies, programs and legislation, including progress toward achieving the objectives and target dates established in the multi-year gender-equality plan.**

E.19 Requiring the deputy ministers of federal departments to be accountable for the implementation of the equality and safety framework. They would be required to allocate resources sufficient for the task and provide their staff with appropriate training, developed in co-operation with the Status of Women ministry.

E.20 Elevating the Sub-Committee on the Status of Women of the Parliamentary Standing Committee on Health and Welfare, Social Affairs, Seniors and Status of Women to full committee status, and requiring its participation in the review of the estimates of all departments to ensure the resource allocations of government appropriately promote women's equality and safety.

Canada's Commitment:

To stimulate the formation and growth of women's organizations and to give financial and organizational support to their activities.

Fulfilling Canada's commitment includes:

E.21 Ensuring the full participation of organizations seeking equality for women, including those representing particularly vulnerable groups, in the formation of public policy by providing adequate, long-term, stable funding.

Canada's Commitment:

To ensure that statistics based on appropriate indicators of women's differential participation in the country's economic structures are available.

Fulfilling Canada's commitment includes:

E.22 Requiring all departments responsible for the compilation and dissemination of statistics to provide data based on gender and other significant demographic characteristics.

E.23 Providing gender-specific data on the impact of economic restructuring.

E.24 Ensuring that Statistics Canada regularly collects and includes data on both the remunerated and unremunerated contributions of women in national economic statistics and in Canada's Gross National Product, especially their contributions to child rearing, caregiving, household, voluntary and community activities. Public policies must be based on this fuller understanding of the social and economic life of the nation.

V   WOMEN AND THE ECONOMY

Women contribute significantly to the Canadian economy through both their paid and unpaid labour. They do not, however, benefit equally from the fruits of their labour. The lower wages paid to women and their status as unpaid workers at home lead to their dependency on the wages and status of their male partners, or relatives. Often the female gender and poverty go together, particularly for older women, women with disabilities and female lone parents.

For Aboriginal women living on reserves or in isolated communities, the barriers to employment are severe. In many cases, these communities do not even have the economic base to provide employment. It will require a concerted effort on the part of the federal government and the Aboriginal leadership to create viable economies to support Aboriginal workers in their own communities. While it is beyond our mandate to resolve this matter, we challenge the federal government and the Aboriginal leadership to address this fundamental issue and to ensure that Aboriginal women are directly involved at every stage in the process.

Women who are financially autonomous in our society are those who are able to benefit from the widest range of options and opportunities. Our recommendations, therefore, work to support women's full participation in the work force and to facilitate their ability to make independent choices.

Key Problems

- Women earn an average of 60¢ for every $1.00 earned by men. [12]

- Underemployment is disproportionately high for women. In addition, there are particular groups of women which are chronically overrepresented among the unemployed and underemployed due to systemic barriers.

- Women are concentrated in a few occupational categories, where they are compressed in the lower levels. [13] Certain women, particularly immigrants, are also concentrated in piecework and domestic work which tend to be non-unionized and pay minimum or below minimum wages. Furthermore, the majority of part-time workers are women. [14]

- Women, particularly immigrants and refugees, often come to Canada as dependants. They enter low-paying jobs or do not work at all, do not have equal access to information about services and programs available to them and may have a cultural heritage which impedes their seeking employment. In addition, many face language barriers or have qualifications which are not recognized in Canada.

- The labour market is often unwilling to recognize the capabilities of women with disabilities or to make adjustments to facilitate their work.

- The labour force participation of women is limited by the fact that they are still the primary caregivers and carry an unfair burden with respect to other domestic duties. Generally, workplace policies and programs are not designed to help balance work and family responsibilities.

- The lack of state support for the costs of child-rearing is a significant barrier for female social assistance recipients who might otherwise enter the work force and reduce their dependency on the state.

- Women do not have the same training, employment and promotion opportunities as men.

- Women are disadvantaged in their old age by lower pensions and income [15] due to non-participation in the paid labour force. Domestic work is not compensated nor used in the calculation of pension credits. The fact that they may have disrupted their careers to have children and to care for family members is not adequately acknowledged or addressed.

- Farm women and other self-employed women operating businesses as independent principals, often face discrimination in their access to financial and other resources necessary for the success of their business ventures.

- Farm women and other women contributing to family-operated businesses are rarely co-owners of business assets or formal partners in the management of enterprises. They seldom have a legal agreement underpinning their business association and do not always receive economic returns (wages, profits, income) in their own right commensurate with their contributions.

- Even when there are employment possibilities in Aboriginal communities, nepotism or favouritism can restrict opportunities for women.

Canada's Commitment:

To provide a range of affordable, accessible and quality child care.

Fulfilling Canada's commitment includes:

E.25 **Implementing a national child care plan based on the principles of equity and flexibility and supported by regulations and standards governing child care workers, programs and facilities.**

E.26 **Ensuring co-ordination among all levels of government with respect to the funding, regulation, taxation and provision of child care.**

E.27 **Encouraging workplace child care services through incentives such as funding, space or tax relief.**

Canada's Commitment:

To ensure public consensus on the need and desirability for women, men and society as a whole to share the responsibilities of raising children and caring for other family members.

Fulfilling Canada's commitment includes:

E.28 **Changing the attitudes and regulations governing maternity and parental leave to ensure that maternity is not treated as an illness; to encourage either parent to take advantage of parental leave; to ensure women and men are treated equally with respect to wage and non-wage benefits or costs; and to remove disincentives such as the current two-week waiting period for receipt of unemployment insurance benefits or the absence of income top-ups above unemployment insurance.**

E.29 Amending provincial and territorial labour standards where necessary to ensure the right to maternity and parental leave for both public and private sector employees.

E.30 Encouraging employers, unions and professional bodies to recognize and support non-work responsibilities by exploring alternative work arrangements with respect to time worked, scheduling and location and developing and implementing workplace education programs to ensure that both women and men take advantage of such arrangements.

Canada's Commitment:

To ensure employment equity for women.

Fulfilling Canada's commitment includes:

E.31 Implementing the recommendations in the report of the Special Committee on the Review of the *Employment Equity Act*, entitled *A Matter of Fairness*.

E.32 Extending the *Employment Equity Act* to cover "more than just numbers." For example, adding measures which would ensure the retention and promotion of women and the fostering of positive work environments.

E.33 Mandating the hiring of a fair percentage of Aboriginal employees, including women, when providing economic assistance to stimulate growth in towns or cities which derive benefit from neighbouring Aboriginal communities.

E.34 Eliminating nepotism and favouritism within Aboriginal governments and programs and ensuring the adherence to fair, competitive recruitment and employment practices, based on merit.

Canada's Commitment:

To guarantee women equal pay for work of equal value.

Fulfilling Canada's commitment includes:

E.35 Developing and implementing pro-active legislation on pay equity including clear guidelines, time frames, scheduled rates of improvement and strong enforcement measures.

Canada's Commitment:

To strengthen training programs for women.

Fulfilling Canada's commitment includes:

E.36 Working with provincial governments to develop a strategy for training and employment to assist female school leavers and women re-entering the work force, to promote occupational desegregation, to help women in declining sectors, to recruit and retain women in high-growth, high-skill, non-traditional and traditional sectors, and to enhance their skills and promote diversification through the use of technology.

E.37 Providing training and skills upgrading, particularly for self-employed women in sectors undergoing rapid restructuring, to ensure that their businesses become or remain competitive.

E.38 Tailoring training to meet women's needs and accommodate their differences with respect to caregiving responsibilities, language abilities, life skills, training hours and location.

E.39 Increasing training funds available to designated groups (women, Aboriginal women, Inuit women, women with disabilities and visible minority women), through the Canadian Jobs Strategy, and, ensuring the equitable participation of designated groups in all labour market adjustment and training programs.

E.40 Reinstating all special needs counsellors and designated group co-ordinators in federal employment and training programs. Their elimination under policy changes has severely reduced access for designated groups to employment counselling and other assistance.

E.41 Ensuring that government-run training and employment programs provide women, young women and other vulnerable groups with access to training programs which promote higher skill levels, such as apprenticeships and workplace-based training, rather than the low-skill training programs which women currently dominate.

E.42 Providing additional resources for training programs and changing the eligibility criteria so they are not limited to those who are currently on unemployment insurance.

Canada's Commitment:

To introduce measures to avoid exploitation of part-time and piece workers, who predominately are women and reduce the trend toward the feminization of part-time, temporary and seasonal work.

Fulfilling Canada's commitment includes:

E.43 Reviewing federal, provincial and territorial labour standards, including an assessment of their application and enforcement. They should be updated, standardized and uniformly applied and enforced.

E.44 Designating home-based workers, including female farm employees, female migrant farm labourers and domestic workers, as employees under federal and provincial labour standards and ensuring, through effective monitoring and enforcement measures, they are covered under the same regulations concerning wages and working conditions as those performing similar work within the regulated workplace.

E.45 Including clauses in all labour legislation providing permanent part-time workers with prorated benefits and ensuring that casual employees are entitled to the same non-wage benefits, on a prorated basis, as permanent staff.

Canada's Commitment:

To introduce measures which recognize the importance of and provide support to women in business, including self-employed women, women traders, women in small industries and women in family enterprises, such as farming.

Fulfilling Canada's commitment includes:

E.46 **Expanding and adequately funding the Farm Women's Advancement Program** [16] **with priority given to funding to improve farm women's economic security and autonomy. This would be done through support to farm women's groups for initiatives to analyze, advocate, consult and increase awareness of farm women's options and legal rights as business partners.**

E.47 **Providing incentives to encourage legally recognized co-ownership and co-management by women of family businesses, including farms.**

E.48 **Implementing a mentor program, similar to the Step-Up Program.** [17] **It would include an ongoing consultant/advisor to provide assistance to participants; selection of successful business women with whom participants would be paired; a training component designed in consultation with participants to develop the knowledge and skills required to start a business or encourage its growth; and a small business loan available upon successful completion of such a program.**

E.49 **Ensuring Aboriginal women have equal access to funds provided for economic development through such programs as the Canadian Aboriginal Economic Development Strategy.** [18]

Canada's Commitment:

To direct special attention, in the provision of social assistance, social services, education, training and employment, to the needs of female victims of violence, female lone parents and women with a high vulnerability to poverty.

Fulfilling Canada's commitment includes:

E.50 **Recognizing the trauma experienced by female victims of violence and developing pre-training programs with counselling to assist them in making the transition into the labour force. Working with women in the shelter or second-stage housing movement to provide employment counselling and assistance to occupants.**

E.51 **Implementing training and employment programs which take into account the full range of barriers to labour force participation facing female victims of violence and female lone parents. This includes the psychological impact of long absences from the labour force, the lack of financial resources, the need for child care, the requirement to have appropriate clothing and equipment and the need for sound advice on career options and progression.**

E.52 **Facilitating and encouraging the labour force participation of female social assistance recipients, particularly female lone parents, by providing a combination of social assistance and training or employment income which ensures a standard of living above the poverty line.**

E.53 **Supplementing the income of older women, who have limited employment prospects but are not yet eligible for retirement benefits, to ensure them a reasonable standard of living.**

VI THE FAMILY

The family is one of the fundamental units of social organization in Canadian society. While family structure can take many forms — extended, nuclear, lone parent, couples of same or opposite sex, with or without children, with or without a formal contract of marriage, etc. — families are generally characterized by varying degrees of material and social interdependency among their members. The nature and degree of dependency can change with age, gender, relationship and status within the family. Roles and functions ascribed to or taken on by various members of the family also differ.

The family itself has been a venue for playing out social and economic inequality on the basis of gender. Historically, biology has been destiny with respect to roles within families. The reproductive function of women has generally been extended to include primary responsibilities for child care and child rearing.

Young children are socialized in the family environment for the gender-based roles they will assume as adolescents and adults. Although some intergenerational shifts in role responsibility occur, family role patterns, reinforced by other institutions such as school, work and the media tend to be repeated from one generation to the next, despite significant economic changes in favour of women and the advent of greater reproductive choice.

Key Problems

- Women assume the bulk of household work, child-rearing and child care responsibilities without monetary compensation.

- Women's discretionary and leisure time declines with marriage and children, particularly if they are employed outside the home, while that of male spouses increases.

- Family dissolution is increasing, and the number of female lone parents living in poverty or near poverty is increasing.

- Different standards for fathers and mothers appear to apply in custody and access decisions.

- Freedom of choice on reproductive matters is sometimes compromised by local limitations, particularly on the availability of abortion.

Canada's Commitment:

To ensure equality during marriage and at its dissolution.

Fulfilling Canada's commitment includes:

E.54 **Recognizing in all aspects of policy the diversity of family structures and composition, and eliminating discrimination arising from the characterization of the family as having a male head of household with a spouse and children in varying states of dependency on the male breadwinner.**

E.55 **Implementing educational programs for men, women, young boys and girls to create greater awareness of shared obligations within the family, particularly responsibilities for child rearing.**

E.56 **Providing child care and after-school care so women as well as men have access to leisure, educational and other personal development activities.**

E.57 **Signing and implementing the International Labour Organization Convention and Recommendation No. 165 regarding access to employment without discrimination arising from family responsibilities.** [19]

E.58 Ensuring that criteria that are free of gender bias are developed and applied to decisions on custody and access.

E.59 Ensuring that child support orders are fairly determined and enforced. This would include consideration of the adoption of an advance payment scheme until such time as universal compliance with spousal and child support orders is achieved.

E.60 Ensuring that the right to reproductive choice and abortion is not compromised.

VII WOMEN AND THE TAX/TRANSFER SYSTEM

Although it does not intentionally set out to discriminate on the basis of gender, the Canadian taxation system reflects and sustains the economic and social structure and, as such, embodies some significant gender biases which work to the disadvantage of women.

As well, the increasing movement away from the corporate sector to income taxes collected from individuals as the major source of government revenues has had a substantial adverse impact on the real income of individuals and families. The regressive nature of some tax measures, such as the child care expense deduction, benefits higher income earners who are more likely to be men. Women, as the greater proportion of lower income earners, must spend more of their income on consumables, and are therefore more adversely affected by consumption taxes such as provincial sales taxes and the goods and services tax.

The direct and indirect costs of raising children and the fact that these costs are borne primarily by women is not adequately recognized in the Canadian tax and social benefits system. This factor, combined with lower wages for work traditionally performed by women, reinforces the assumption that children are the responsibility of the mother and tends, therefore, to justify her temporary absences from the labour market.

Under the Canadian system, married partners are treated as a unit for some tax purposes. The presumption that income is equally shared within families is false. Current policy can create disincentives for the higher income-earning spouse, usually male, to have his spouse in the paid labour force, even while strong economic incentives may exist for her to do so in order to achieve and maintain her economic autonomy.

Key Problems

- Female lone parents, who are among the lowest income earners, receive limited support through the tax system because the primary tax benefit available to them, the equivalent-to-married credit, is non-refundable.

- Child care is subsidized through deductions rather than benefits or credits. This increases the tax benefit for those most able to pay.

- The lack of full indexation of child benefit payments and child-related tax credits (such as the GST credit per child), erodes their value over time.

- Canadian tax policy does not take into account the impact of tax measures on individuals on the basis of gender.

- The taxation of child-support payments, while containing elements of fairness in theory, is complex and often inappropriately implemented. This reduces the financial resources allocated to the custodial parent (usually the mother) in the interests of the child.

- Tax benefits from contributions to RRSPs and private pension plans benefit higher income earners and long-term labour market participants. As a result, women are placed at a disadvantage.

Canada's Commitment:

To take all appropriate measures, including legislation, to modify or abolish existing laws, regulations, customs and practices which constitute discrimination against women. [20]

Fulfilling Canada's commitment includes:

E.61 **Analyzing all proposed tax system changes for bias or adverse effects based on gender.**

E.62 **Acknowledging through the tax system the costs of raising children and the reduced capacity of families with children to pay taxes. This includes raising the income level threshold at which the child benefit is reduced, fully indexing all credits and benefits under the new federal child benefit program and increasing the maximum deductions under the child care expense deduction and making it convertible to a refundable credit.**

E.63 **Treating spouses as individuals for tax purposes by abolishing the married and equivalent-to-married credits, and replacing them with new measures which explicitly recognize the costs of raising children, including refundable tax credits for low earner parents, particularly lone parents.**

E.64 **Addressing the taxation and collection problems in the current child support order system by introducing a tax credit approach, and using the tax collection system as a means for enforcing child support payments.**

E.65 **Fully indexing income tax brackets.**

E.66 **Increasing and fully indexing the clawback threshold for OAS benefits.**

E.67 **Making automatic the credit-splitting provisions of the CPP for ex-spouses.**

ENDNOTES

1 *The Nairobi Forward-looking Strategies for the Advancement of Women*, (Ottawa, 19), p.7. Reprinted by Status of Women Canada from the *Report of the World Conference to Review and Appraise the acheivements of the United Nations Decade for Women: Equality, Development and Peace* (United Nations Document A/Conf.116/28)

2 *Universal Declaration of Human Rights* as reprinted by Multiculturalism and Citizenship Canada, Human Rights Directorate in *Observance of Human Rights Day December 10, 1988: The 40th Anniversary of the Universal Declaration of Human Rights 1948-1988:Report of Canada to the United Nations* (Ottawa, 1989)

3 *Convention on the Elimination of All Forms of Discrimination against Women* as reprinted by the Human Rights Directorate Multiculturalism and Citizenship Canada, with the permission of the Department of Public Information of the United Nations, (Ottawa, 1990)

4 General recommendation No. 19 (Eleventh session, 1992) as reprinted in Arvonne Fraser and Miranta Kazantsis, *International Women's Rights Action Watch:(IWRAW) CEDAW #11* (University of Minnesota, 1992), pp. 28-32.

5 Unless otherwise specified, the Panel has excerpted "Canada's Commitment" statements from the Status of Women publication entitled, *Fact Sheets: Nairobi Forward-looking Strategies for the Advancement of Women, Issues and the Canadian Situation*, (Ottawa: 1992). The Fact Sheets summarize the *Nairobi Forward-looking Strategies*, in point form, by issue, and offer current information on Canadian government action towards equality.

6 The Court Challenges Program was a federal initiative which provided financial assistance to selected individuals and groups to litigate equality rights cases relating to federal legislation, practices or policies under section 15 of the *Charter*. The program was designed to provide access to the courts for women and other minority groups. It was cut in the 1992 federal budget, despite the protests of equality rights advocates.

7 Minister of Supply and Sevices Canada, The Report of the Task Force on Barriers to Women in the Public Service, *Beneath the Veneer*, (Ottawa, 1990), pp. 37-38.

8 Minister of Supply and Sevices Canada, The Report of the Special Committee on the Review of the *Employment Equity Act, A Matter of Fairness*, (Ottawa, 1992), pp. 2-4.

9 *Ibid.*, p. 3.

10 Minister of Supply and Sevices Canada,The Report of the Royal Commission on Electoral Reform and Party Financing, *Reforming Electoral Democracy*, (Ottawa, 1991).

11 *Beneath the Veneer, op. cit.*, p. 9.

12 Abdul Rashid, "Seven decades of wage changes," in *Perspectives on Labour and Income*, Volume 5, No.2, Summer 1993, p.13.

13 Nancy Zukewich Graham, "Women in the Workplace," in *Canadian Social Trends*, No. 28, Spring 1993, pp. 4-5.

14 *Ibid.*, p. 3.

15 Statistics Canada, *Women in Canada - A Statistical Report* (Ministry of Supply and Services, 2nd edition, Ottawa, 1990), pp. 121-124.

16 The Farm Women's Advancement Program was developed in 1988, by the Farm Women's Bureau of Agriculture Canada. Its objectives are: to aid in the achievement of legal and economic equality for farm women; promote the participation of farm women in the agricultural industry's decision-making processes; and, encourage the recognition of the contribution of farm women to the well-being of the agricultural sector.

17 The Step-Up Program is a business expansion program for women in Ontario, sponsored by the Federal Business Development Bank and the Ontario Ministry of Industry, Trade and Technology. It provides the skills women need to expand their enterprises. It was piloted from April 1991 to April 1992 with 25 protegees and 25 mentors.

18 The Canadian Aboriginal Economic Development Strategy is a federal initiative designed to provide long-term employment and business opportunities to Canada's Aboriginal citizens, by giving them the means to effectively manage their own business enterprises, economic institutions, job training and skills development.

19 Recommendation No. 165 as found in *International Labour Organisation,* International Labour Conventions and Recommendations 1919-1991, Volume II (Geneva, 1992), pp. 1248-1254

20 *Convention on the Elimination of all Forms of Discrimination against Women, op. cit*, p. 6.

SECTION 2

ZERO TOLERANCE POLICY

The Context

1. Male violence against women is at a crisis level in Canada and must be urgently addressed.

2. Violence against women is a violation of a most basic human right to security of the person.

3. Violence against women is a manifestation of historically unequal power relations between men and women. This unequal relationship has led to domination over and discrimination against women by men, endangering women and preventing their full advancement in society.

4. Violence against women is one of the crucial social mechanisms by which women are forced into a position subordinate to men.

5. Violence against women is a product of a sexist, racist, heterosexist and class society and is perpetuated through all social institutions and the attitudes and behaviours of members of all Canadian communities.

6. Violence against women is an abuse of power and a betrayal of trust. It precludes the establishment of egalitarian relations and inhibits the mutual respect that women have a right to expect as individuals and as a social group.

7. Violence affects women's abilities to exercise freedom in their homes, workplaces, on the streets and in their communities.

8. Organizations, institutions and governments do not effectively detect and deter violence against women and thereby perpetuate the abuse of women and endanger their safety.

9. The statistical rate of repeat offences is very high for crimes of violence against women, and society puts women at risk by denying this fact.

10. Violence against women includes various types of abuse — psychological, financial, verbal, sexual and physical. It affects all women but with different consequences for Aboriginal and Inuit women, young women, elderly women, women of colour, immigrant women, refugee women, domestic workers, women with disabilities, women from different linguistic backgrounds, women living in rural, northern and isolated communities and lesbians.

11. Much of the violence against women is preventable, but society has not taken the appropriate measures to guarantee women's safety.

12. The severe and costly impact of violence on women, both physical and psychological, can also be measured in terms of lost potential and damage to children.

Declaration

The Canadian Panel on Violence Against Women declares:

- Equality and freedom from violence are rights of all women, and it is the responsibility of every individual, community, government and institution in Canada to work toward securing these rights.

- The elimination of violence will best be achieved through the adoption and rigorous application of a policy of zero tolerance.

- To this end we urge each person and every organization in Canada to commit to the equality and safety of women and implement the Zero Tolerance Policy.

Zero tolerance is based on the following principles.

1. No amount of violence is acceptable, and the elimination of violence against women must be an absolute priority.

2. Those with responsibility for public safety have an obligation to take the most comprehensive and effective action possible to prevent violence from happening and to limit the harms from violence when it has occurred.

3. Policies, practices, programs and products which do not support women's safety must be dismantled.

4. Sexist and racist practices and other forms of discrimination and bias which encourage or support acts of violence against women must be eliminated.

5. The rights of the victim in the legal system must at least be equal to the rights of the accused.

6. Victims must not be blamed for the violence committed against them.

7. Governments and institutions have a primary responsibility to demonstrate leadership and to provide resources to achieve equality and to end violence.

8. Individuals and all communities within Canadian society have a responsibility to work toward ending violence and achieving equality for all.

The Policy Framework of Zero Tolerance

Adoption of the Zero Tolerance Policy means making a firm commitment to the philosophy that no amount of violence is acceptable, and that adequate resources must be made available to eliminate violence and achieve equality.

The elimination of violence against women can only be achieved through recognition of the equality of women. Equality initiatives will enhance women's options and reduce their vulnerability to violence.

Ending Violence ⟷ Equality
Zero Tolerance Policy ⟷ Equality Plan

To this end, a separate equality action plan has been developed which includes mechanisms to assist government in ensuring that all policies, practices and programs embody the principles of equality for women. These initiatives will support groups, organizations and institutions in achieving their goal of equality for women.

The policy framework for zero tolerance outlined below complements the equality action plan. It includes:

- an accountability framework which identifies criteria for zero tolerance to help an organization change its operations by making the elimination of violence and support for women's safety integral to all its activities;

- an outline of steps to be taken in implementing the Zero Tolerance Policy;

- a model for organizations or institutions to use as a guide to implementing the zero tolerance criteria to change business practices.

Institutions can use the Zero Tolerance Policy to examine their operations for the degree to which they support women's safety, enhance or promote women's equality, and are sensitive to gender issues.

The Zero Tolerance Policy is generic and is equally relevant to support groups, non-government organizations, services, corporations and government institutions.

Accountability Framework

The following criteria are to be used to shape the work to be undertaken and to evaluate progress made in reaching zero tolerance. All criteria apply to any activity carried out and to evaluations of progress.

All activities must unequivocally support and promote women's safety and security through:

Eliminating gender, race and class bias

- by identifying and eliminating any element or underlying assumption that undermines women, for example, myths, stereotypes or roles, based on gender, race or class;

- by recognizing women's realities and experiences as different from those of men; and

- by introducing measures that further equality.

Ending violence

- by supporting victims and redressing harms when violence occurs;

- by implementing policies and practices that ensure women's safety; and

- by identifying and eliminating problem areas and situations, including at all work sites, that create danger or promote or tolerate violent actions or harassment for women within the organization.

Ensuring inclusion

- by recognizing the interconnections between the structures of economic power and the organization of elite white male power in society;

- by basing decision making on data and research that accurately reflect women's safety, different realities, experiences and perspectives; and

- by engaging, at each and every stage of all activities, the full participation of women who represent the diversity of Canada and who have direct experience, working knowledge and a demonstrated commitment to equality and ending violence.

Implementation Steps

To apply the Zero Tolerance Policy, a group, organization or institution has six major steps to take:

1.   Commit

Formally adopt the Zero Tolerance Policy on violence.   Communicate to every member and client/consumer of the organization that women's safety is a priority, and no amount of violence is acceptable.

2.   Committee

Create a zero tolerance action committee to oversee implementation with membership that includes senior management and a majority of women drawn from all areas and all levels of the organization who represent employees/workers, management, unions and client/consumer groups.

3.   Review

Undertake safety audits of work sites, physical plants as well as of policies, practices, procedures and programs, to detect and deal with situations and employees/workers posing a risk to women's safety.

4.   Act

Develop an action plan to detect, deter and prevent violence against women and to ensure women's safety in all aspects of operations and products. Benchmarks and timetables should be built in, and all stakeholders should be directly involved in the plan's development and implementation.

5. Resource

Ensure that the zero tolerance action committee has adequate human and financial resources to be effective. Allocate funds for implementation of the action plan.

6. Evaluate

The zero tolerance action committee must oversee the adoption of and adherence to the Zero Tolerance Policy, must ensure ongoing monitoring and evaluation of the progress made and must report on achievements in their annual report.

Zero Tolerance Model

The following model focuses on the specific aspects of an organization's operations and work; it should be reviewed and realigned using the zero tolerance criteria. Actions are recommended to guide the evaluation and reformulation of operational activities.

A. Priority Setting/Allocation of Resources

A.1   Statement of Commitment

A written commitment to the promotion of women's equality and safety must be included when developing goals, objectives or mission statements, undertaking strategic planning exercises and setting priorities.

The statement is the formal recognition of women's equal access to all resources, programs and information. It is based on women's experiences and realities including those of victims and survivors.

A.2   Funding

Women's equality and safety needs must be considered in the design of budgets, including core funding, subsidies and grants. The model requires institutions and organizations to account for funding as follows:

- Compensate the value of women's contributions adequately.

- Grant fiscal resources to institutions, agencies or organizations conditional on their adoption of the Zero Tolerance Policy. To facilitate compliance, human and/or financial resources should be provided, where possible, to support the development of action plans and the achievement of a zero tolerance commitment.

B. Human Resource Management

B.1   Appointments and Hiring

The intensity of the screening process for appointments and hiring must increase in proportion to the degree of trust or power inherent in the position, especially if the position involves access to children or adults who are vulnerable. Priority must be given to the following hiring criteria to ensure women's safety.

- Through an in-depth check of references and background, confirm that there is no evidence that a prospective employee or appointee would pose a safety risk to co-workers or clients/consumers. The onus is on the candidate to disclose previous criminal convictions.

- Demonstrated understanding of equality issues and the dynamics of violence.

- Personal support of and commitment to women's equality and safety.

B.2   Performance Review and Promotions

Promotions should be based on several factors:

- There are no reasonable and probable grounds for concern that the individual would pose a safety risk or tolerate violence against women.

- The individual has not demonstrated sexist or other discriminatory attitudes, behaviours, or tolerance of violence against women.

- Training on issues of women's safety and equality has been completed, and understanding of that training has been demonstrated.

- Power, authority and trust have been used appropriately by the individual.

- The individual supports and is committed to women's safety and equality.

- The individual conforms to workplace policies on violence, including harassment.

B.3   Training

All employees/workers must receive proper training on woman abuse, sexism and racism. In-depth training must be given to all senior staff; to individuals specifically involved in any process to address complaints or solve problems related to women's safety and equality; to individuals who implement policies and procedures; and to individuals who make decisions on the allocation of resources or assess service/program delivery.

Curricula must be developed and delivered in partnership with individuals who have expertise in working with equality issues and violence against women.

Training on violence against women issues must be integrated into all existing courses and curricula, rather than given as a single course.

Basic training must cover the nature and harms of inequality and discrimination; the incidence of women abuse; the specific situations and circumstances of women survivors; the characteristics and consequences of violence against women; all forms of violence; sexism; racism; the needs of women with disabilities, elderly women and lesbians; the ways a victim may initiate disclosure or inquiry; barriers to disclosure and how to respond appropriately; violence prevention training, such as non-violent and non-discriminatory methods of resolving conflicts; and self-defence training given by women's organizations.

In-depth training must recognize the risk of harm posed by abusers, including those abusing through a breach of trust; difficulties in identifying and helping abusers; and the potential abuse of survivors' rights and safety in investigation and adjudication processes.

B.4   Personnel Policies

Develop and implement comprehensive personnel policies on issues related to women's equality, including employment equity and pay equity; women's safety, including sexual harassment, gender discrimination and violence prevention; and support for victims.

A policy on harassment must consider women's objective and subjective experiences and the intent of the harasser. The policy must identify complaint, grievance and investigative procedures, and redress responsibilities including disciplinary action to be taken to resolve the complaint.

- Make it easy for victims to report.

- Define sexual harassment and recognize that gender harassment, which can undermine the business or service delivery atmosphere, is as harmful a form of sexual harassment as the more commonly recognized forms.

- Include a step-by-step strategy for recognizing, investigating and resolving incidents of sexual harassment.

- Resolve complaints without delay and in a manner which protects the confidentiality of complainants.

- Provide for facts to be accurately recorded, kept on file for a significant time period and held in strict confidence.

- Ensure that remedial action is taken immediately (i.e., under three months) that satisfies and never penalizes the victim.

- Provide measures for separating parties during the complaint procedure, if necessary, but never to the detriment of the victim.

- Provide outside legal counsel who have an understanding and concern for women's safety issues.

- Ensure that punishment/restitution reflects the severity of the crime.

- Include dismissal in the policy as the most severe penalty for harassment.

- Leave policies must be developed or amended to support victims of violence who are absent from work due to violence.

- Grant leave for victims of abuse, and for parents of children who have been abused and who require time off for counselling, support, court appearances and other related activities.

- Guarantee the positions of employees/workers who have been victims of violence upon return from leave.

- Employee assistance programs must support employees/workers who may be victims of violence and refer them to appropriate community support services.

- Dismissal of staff or appointees who do not comply with behaviour or harassment policies and/or who commit acts of violence must be ensured.

C.   Legislation/Regulation/Policy

C.1   Acts, statutes, by-laws, registries, codes in development and the granting of licences must uphold and protect women's safety and security. This includes protection from further abuse by individuals or systems. They must also recognize women's different needs and realities.

D. Programs/Services/Practices

D.1 Safety/prevention practices and programs that recognize and eliminate the opportunities for abuse and violence within an organization must be considered when drafting guidelines and directives supporting the organization's mandate.

- Develop protocols for workers/employees to use to recognize and confront violence by a colleague or in potentially violent situations.

- Inform workers/employees about available support which can be given to women experiencing violence.

- Post signs stating that acts of violence including sexual and gender harassment, racism and other forms of discrimination may result in the perpetrator being fired.

E. Consultation

E.1 The following criteria must be considered when setting up committees, advisory bodies, councils or activities such as hearings.

- Invite a proportional number of women representing specific groups of the community to participate.

- Incorporate the expertise and experiences provided by participants in all planning, program/service activities and human resource practices.

F. Co-ordination

F.1 All parties, processes, activities and projects on the same or related subject areas must co-operate and collaborate to make links among issues where the relationship to equality and violence is less apparent.

G. Research and Evaluation

G.1 Research undertaken through pilot projects, experimentation and the resulting data collection and analysis must reflect the priorities of women. It must be measured against its contribution to women's equality and women's safety; give equal recognition of and support to feminist research methodology; and include specific gender and race breakdowns.

G.2 Self-evaluation is a requisite element in assessing the effectiveness and success of any policy, practice, program or service in reaching equality and promoting women's safety. At a minimum, self-evaluation must include the following activities.

- Gauge and take into account the different impact of each activity on women and men.

- Examine and evaluate how the specific needs of women are being addressed.

- Evaluate how existing resources can be redirected to respond to the identified needs.

H. Education/Promotional Activities

H.1 Awareness campaigns, publications, advertising and other communications products must include the following activities.

- Adopt non-sexist/non-racist images and verbal communications which portray women in the full range of occupations and reflect all client groups.

- Give equal value to women's experiences and needs.

- Provide all materials in culturally relevant, plain language, in a range of media (including large print and braille) and where necessary, provide linguistic and sign language interpretation.

- Promote non-violent images and messages in support of women's safety and security.

I. Physical Environment Management

I.1 Support for women's safety and security must be reflected in the physical design of facilities and maintenance of properties including public and semi-public spaces such as parks, shopping malls, public transit systems, workplaces, and public buildings.

- Provide for women's safety during any construction and renovation.

- Support women's safety through provisions in by-laws and other legislation regulating municipally operated spaces such as underground garages.

- Increase the safety and security of isolated working conditions through the use of regular patrols and communication devices.

- Ensure escape routes.

J. Accountability

J.1 In working in or dealing with an organization, women workers/employees, women clients and consumers must be guaranteed that their safety and security will be upheld.

- Work in an open and transparent manner.

- Disclose information about processes and objectives freely.

- Invite public scrutiny of work.

- Keep the public and all stakeholders informed on progress.

- Adopt a code of behaviour which emphasizes non-sexist, non-racist and other non-discriminatory behaviour and which includes a sexual harassment policy as well as a complaints process. The complaints process must guarantee that all complaints are documented and investigated within a reasonable time period. Penalties and remedies that recognize the harms done to the victim must also be defined.

- Review policies, procedures, practices, programs, services or activities undertaken by the zero tolerance action committee annually to assess and publicly report on the organization's performance in reaching zero tolerance.

SECTION 3

ZERO TOLERANCE ACTION PLANS

In this section, we recommend specific actions to be undertaken in key sectors which complement the adoption and implementation of the Zero Tolerance Policy. The eight sectors are:

- Services (Health and Social)
- Legal
- Workplace
- Military
- Education
- Media
- Religious Institutions
- Government

Actions in each sector are stated as recommendations and may be aimed at several actors within the sector or at specific individuals, organizations or institutions. Given the complexity of some sectors and the scope of changes required to redress historical inequities, some recommendations may be accompanied by further details explaining the intent and nature of the action to be taken in the particular area.

For ease of reference, we have organized the recommended actions into two categories.

- New orientations are fundamental shifts to the individual sector. Once implemented they will support equality and create safety and security for women.

- Zero Tolerance Actions are addressed to all or to specific actors in individual sectors. These are presented according to the 10 activity areas highlighted in the Zero Tolerance Policy:

A. **Priority Setting/Allocation of Resources**
B. **Human Resource Management**
C. **Legislation/Regulation/Policy**
D. **Programs/Services/Practices**
E. **Consultation**
F. **Co-ordination**
G. **Research and Evaluation**
H. **Education/Promotional Activities**
I. **Physical Environment Management**
J. **Accountability**

Only those activity areas requiring attention by specific individuals, institutions or organizations have been included for each sector. For activity areas not specifically addressed, individuals, institutions and organizations should refer to the generic recommended actions under the same activity heading in the Zero Tolerance Policy.

The Panel proposes that all actions begin immediately, with results to be achieved by the year 2000. In some instances, more specific time frames are suggested.

SERVICES SECTOR

Introduction

Services are critical to the women and children victims and survivors of violence and are often the very first point of contact for women seeking information, support and advice. A broad definition of the services sector has been adopted for this action plan to reflect the results of the Panel's consultations. It includes settings and service providers from the social/community services and health care fields. Specifically, the following key participants have been identified:

- non-governmental services including shelters, sexual assault centres, rape crisis centres, women's centres, men's programs and other community groups;

- governmental services including social service agencies, hospitals and medical clinics;

- self-regulating bodies and professional associations;

- physicians, psychiatrists, other health practitioners such as nurses, psychologists, therapists and counsellors;

- ministries of social and/or community services;

- ministries of health; and

- federal government departments responsible for health, welfare, social services, Indian and Northern Affairs, and other relevant federal government departments.

Key Problems

Approaches to the needs of victims and survivors and subsequent interventions are changing. Nevertheless, key problems remain in both the delivery and the basic philosophy that underpin the services sector.

- The lack of stable and ongoing funding for non-governmental services has created gaps in the overall network of service delivery, particularly for shelters and second-stage housing. Women working in community-based organizations are poorly paid and have very little job security.

- The needs of certain populations of women, such as Aboriginal and Inuit women, women with disabilities, immigrant women, women of colour, refugee women, domestic workers, lesbians, rural women, young women, elderly women and women from linguistic minorities are not being adequately met.

- The needs of children including those who have witnessed violence are often neglected because of funding inadequacies and the lack of recognition that the witnessing of abuse is in itself a type of abuse.

- A wide range of programs, services and counselling techniques are currently employed in responding to victims and survivors. Many of these services work independently, and the lack of a common approach or orientation creates an uneven and unco-ordinated response, sending an unclear message to both the men who commit the violence and the women who survive it.

- The bio-medical approach practised in health care separates the human body from its social environment. For women survivors of violence this means that the issue of violence is isolated from its context, and, in effect, makes them responsible for their condition.

• Health care practice also tends to ignore the link between the mind and the body. Consequently, the multi-faceted nature of violence is not recognized. Violence is often considered an illness requiring a medical response. The symptoms of violence are the only focus; the underlying causes are ignored. Survivors are attended to with medication or considered mentally ill and referred for psychiatric treatment.

New Orientations

The federal government and provincial/ territorial ministries of social and/or community services.

S.1 **Provide ongoing funding to all services for short-, medium- and long-term planning. Core funding is recommended for community-based, non-governmental services such as women's shelters, sexual assault centres, rape crisis centres and women's centres. Sustained funding is recommended for government agencies and institutionally based services. Some experimentation through pilot projects should be employed to investigate ways of expanding both the community-based and government-based service networks.**

Details

Funding must be at a level which allows all services to be culturally relevant and to provide accessibility to all women in the community.

The allocation of funding must provide for fair and equitable compensation and benefits to workers in the community sector and for staff training and development needs.

Funding must provide for the expansion of services in both non-governmental and governmental service networks. For shelters, specifically, the following additional services should be accommodated:

• *minimum stay of 30 days followed by an evaluation of the client's needs for her future;*

• *counselling and support groups for children;*

• *temporary accommodation for victims of sexual assault;*

• *development and co-ordination of satellite houses and other services in remote and isolated communities;*

• *second-stage housing; and*

• *educational/advocacy activities.*

The following additional services/programs are recommended for government service agencies:

• *multi-disciplinary teams in institutionalized settings;*

• *peer support counselling programs;*

• *self-help groups;*

• *family support services;*

• *short- and long-term counselling for children including children's groups;*

• *offenders groups; and*

• *services for adolescent offenders.*

Provincial/territorial ministries of health, and the federal department responsible for health.

S.2   There must be a major reorientation of the philosophy underpinning health care delivery from that of piecemeal treatment to a comprehensive model of healing which considers the person as a whole and understands the multi-faceted nature of violence and the complex ways in which all its dimensions — physical, sexual, psychological and social — interact.

S.3   There must be a recognition of the essential contribution made to the healing process of survivors by services delivered at the community level which are not medically oriented and not attached to institutions such as hospitals or clinics. This includes contributions by self-help groups, immigrant health services and other culturally appropriate services. Such a recognition will require a significant re-allocation of financial resources to these community-based services.

Federal departments responsible for health, welfare and social services, provincial-teritorial ministries of social and/or community services, and health, professional associations, frontline workers, social workers, other service providers.

S.4   To ensure completeness, continuity, consistency and quality of service delivery, national standards must be developed and established for the provision of adequate services.

Details

Examples of such standards could include:

*   *a crisis line in each community (a toll-free 1-800 number in remote and isolated communities);*

*   *a counsellor in each community with knowledge of all forms of violence against women and of specialized services and community support services to respond to these needs;*

*   *an emergency shelter or services within one hour commuting distance of each community;*

*   *local, safe, pre-arranged transportation in each community to reach the shelter or other community services;*

*   *integrated approaches to counselling to provide help to both the victim (including children) and the offender on a separate basis but within a global feminist intervention framework. Co-ordination would be ensured by the respective service providers; and*

*   *protocols and procedures to assist in detecting physical, sexual and emotional abuse in victims of violence.*

S.5 All services dealing with Aboriginal and Inuit communities must acknowledge and work to alleviate the underlying social factors that directly contribute to alcohol, drug and solvent use. Additional supports, as identified by communities, must be made immediately available until such time as sufficient education, employment/economic base and adequate housing are in place to alleviate those underlying causes.

Communities across Canada.

S.6 Each community must establish a standing committee to co-ordinate services to survivors/victims of violence against women. Membership must include primary providers of service to women and children who have experienced violence – shelters, rape crisis centres, women's centres, social services, police and hospitals/nursing stations. There must be equal participation of community services, government agencies and institutionalized services.

Start-up costs and sufficient funds must be provided for administration and ongoing human resource requirements.

In Inuit and Aborigional communities, this committee would act as a liaison mechanism and pursue complaints pertaining to services.

Zero Tolerance Actions for all Organizations and Individuals in the Services Sector

Priority Setting/Allocation of Resources

S.7 Subscribe to a client-centred model of service delivery. This means that services exist to meet the needs of clients/survivors and not those of service providers. Such an approach strives to redress the power imbalance between the client/survivor and the service provider and enables clients to have input into and control over the development and delivery of services. This ensures that clients/survivors have access to information to assist them in making choices.

Accountability

S.8 Adopt a code of ethics based on the Zero Tolerance Policy that guarantees the rights to dignity, respect, confidentiality, safety and security.

Details

Adherence to the code must be ensured through:

* *the adoption of a comprehensive strategy for educating service providers and users about the philosophical underpinnings, the values and the principles inherent in the code;*

* *performance reviews;*

* *strong sanctions (warnings, missed opportunities for promotion, dismissal, suspension of licence) for violating the code; and*

* *effective complaint procedures.*

Local women's organizations that represent the diverse realities of women and have expertise in this area must be involved.

Zero Tolerance Actions for Specific Organizations

All non-governmental services including shelters, sexual assault centres, rape crisis centres, women's centres, men's programs and other community groups and governmental services including social service agencies, hospitals, community health agencies and medical clinics.

Priority Setting/Allocation of Resources

S.9 **Re-direct existing resources to make services more culturally sensitive and more accessible.**

Details

- *providing linguistic and cultural interpretation;*

- *keeping service providers informed about changes in immigration and refugee laws and policies; and*

- *making traditional healing practices available to Aboriginal women.*

Services to facilitate accessibility could include:

- *making child care more available;*

- *providing physical accessibility and making available new technology, such as TDD phones and ASL interpreters, that enable people with sight and hearing loss to use the services;*

- *accommodating the special needs of women with psychiatric disabilities;*

- *making specialized counsellors/resource individuals available (whether on site or through referrals) to Aboriginal women, Inuit women, women of colour, immigrant women, refugee women, women with disabilities, elderly women and lesbians;*

- *providing counselling services in small Inuit communities in conjunction with services such as health, crafts or recreation to provide increased anonymity and confidentiality;*

- *responding to the needs of women involved in pornography and prostitution through crisis intervention services, referral services, support and counselling, and where possible, shelter;*

- *providing services that recognize the needs of lesbians; and*

- *responding to the needs of women in the military, as dependants and as personnel, through support and information about their rights and access to financial resources.*

Human Resource Management

S.10 **Recruit survivors who have previously used the services and who are healed.**

S.11 **Provide specialized training on the needs of women with disabilities, elderly women, Aboriginal women, Inuit women, immigrant women, women of colour and refugee women; on the power imbalance and trust inherent in any relationship between a service provider and a client; and on feminist intervention skills.**

Co-ordination

S.12 Adopt a co-operative working partnership with legal and other services directly involved with survivors of violence. This partnership would be grounded in mutual respect and recognition of each other's value and expertise. To achieve this, procedures and protocols must be established to identify gaps, solve problems, avoid duplication and share expertise; and linkages must be maintained with all sectors of the community (schools, businesses, other community organizations, religious institutions and other agencies), so these sectors can remain current on resources and can draw on available expertise.

Research and Evaluation

S.13 Undertake the systematic collection of data to determine the needs and percentage of users by forms of violence and populations.

All self-regulating bodies and professional associations.

Legislation/Regulation/Policy

S.14 Improve access to formal complaints and discipline procedures for victims and survivors.

Details

This can be accomplished by:

- ensuring that a complainant's letter is not sent to the health practitioner or service provider without the complainant's explicit knowledge and consent;

- granting the complainant the right to intervene in a disciplinary hearing; and

- establishing criteria for expert testimony.

Programs/Services/Practices

S.15 Improve or develop standardized protocols and procedures to assist professionals in detecting physical, sexual and psychological abuse in survivors.

Details

Examples include:

- explaining how to create the opportunity for clients to disclose their abuse in private without the presence of a partner;

- demonstrating how to assess the extent, severity and duration of the violence by asking non-directed, non-threatening and non-judgmental questions;

- recommending, as normal follow-up procedure, the immediate referral of clients to appropriate community support services;

- *recommending that detailed records be kept of injuries and conditions of abused clients detected as a result of a thorough physical examination, including injuries that might be considered minor, such as scratches and bruises, which could be used as medical evidence in the event of subsequent legal proceedings;*

- *recommending the setting of appropriate boundaries between the practitioner and a client; and*

- *recommending trauma healing and counselling for sexual assault as a priority when seeing newly arrived refugee women, especially if torture is indicated or suspected.*

Research and Evaluation

S.16 Undertake research to evaluate the effectiveness, efficiency and efficacy of the roles of professionals in addressing the needs of women who experience violence.

S.17 Review or encourage the development of new screening or diagnostic tools to assist professionals in making links between past or present problems of violence and various conditions suffered by women such as depression, anorexia and bulimia.

Education/Promotional Activities

S.18 Undertake a public education program which includes:

- the existence and the role of the self-regulating body, its complaints process and how to access the system; and

- examples of abusive behaviours, the warning signs that violence by a health practitioner or service provider may occur and how to get help after being abused, including the necessary procedures for reporting abuse perpetrated by health practitioners and service providers.

S.19 Provide all clients with accessible information in plain language on clients' rights, the necessary procedures for reporting abuse by professionals and service providers and the effects of prescribed drugs.

All health practitioners including physicians, psychiatrists, nurses, psychologists, therapists.

Programs/Services/Practices

S.20 Follow a feminist intervention approach with the appropriate use of medical and psychiatric services.

S .21 Make links between past or present experiences of violence and various conditions suffered by women such as depression, anorexia or bulimia.

Co-ordination

S.22 Liaise with community services, such as transition houses, police and social service agencies, through participation in interagency committees on violence against women or other co-ordinating mechanisms within the community.

All ministries of social and/or community services.

Priority Setting/Allocation of Resources

S.23 Continue to recognize and financially support the efforts undertaken by community organizations to pursue the development of services relevant to violence against women. These efforts could include educational programs and materials for such groups as Aboriginal women, immigrant women, refugee women, women from linguistic minorities and women with disabilities, and the translation of such materials.

S.24 Support only those programs for men which have adopted a policy of zero tolerance, whose clients have been sentenced and which have involved the participation of local women's groups working with women survivors.

S.25 Allocate resources equitably between services working with women survivors and those working with offenders.

S.26 Implement contract compliance in funding and granting powers to institutions and agencies such as social service agencies. Funds or grants would be conditional depending on adoption of a zero tolerance policy and a commitment to participate in a community-based and co-ordinated response to violence against women.

S.27 Ensure that funding for initiatives to prevent violence against women in Aboriginal and Inuit communities comprise a portion of all service delivery contracts and contribution agreements.

S.28 Simplify application, proposal and reporting procedures to allow greatest access to funds by community groups. Liaison personnel must be made available to provide training in proposal writing, access to information on government funding, etc.

Human Resource Management

S.29 Establish registries of professionals with expertise in various forms of violence including sexual abuse, elder abuse, ritual abuse and feminist intervention skills. These registries should be available to interdisciplinary teams and services working in the field of violence against women.

Legislation/Regulation/Policy

S.30 Develop policies to end violence against women from a zero tolerance and equality perspective and not from a family violence perspective.

S.31 Assist women victims of violence in regaining economic independence by:

- recognizing the time needed to heal;

- amending relevant legislation and regulation to ensure that welfare assistance not be reduced in cases where support payments are also received; and by

- providing comprehensive pre-employment training.

S.32 Establish registries to monitor service providers found guilty of breach of confidentiality, breach of trust or convicted of sexual assault, sexual harassment or woman abuse.

S.33 Recognize that a child who has witnessed the abuse of a mother is an abused child and requires appropriate support services.

S.34 Protect Aboriginal and Inuit children in a culturally appropriate way. To achieve this, efforts must be made to keep children in safe and healthy Inuit and Aboriginal settings that reflect their cultural identity.

Programs/Services/Practices

S.35 Amend all procedures and protocols used by social service providers in their work with women victims of violence to reflect a gender, race and class analysis.

S.36 Recognize, as a legitimate social work practice, the use of a feminist intervention approach by service providers working in government settings. Encourage its adoption as a standard approach.

S.37 Acknowledge the experience and analysis of front-line workers by using them as paid trainers, paid expert witnesses, paid educators and paid consultants to provide input in program development and implementation.

S.38 Give serious consideration to supporting services initiated by, developed by and tailored to the specific needs of immigrant women, refugee women and women of colour.

S.39 Disseminate information on availability of government programs to community service providers, in the language appropriate to the community.

Consultation

S.40 Establish a permanent advisory committee to collaborate with government in reviewing and approving funding proposals from community organizations and government institutions and agencies for projects concerning violence against women.

Details

The committee would also monitor and assist in integrating into the government policy-making process, the work accomplished by government-funded projects dealing with violence against women. Survivors, front-line workers and women of all groups would be represented.

Co-ordination

S.41 Recognize and encourage social service workers to network and co-operate with front-line workers, health practitioners, community service workers and to participate in interagency committees on violence against women or other community co-ordinating mechanisms.

S.42 Promote co-operation and collaboration among all parties, all processes and all activities and projects in government settings related to violence against women and to equality.

S.43 Ensure that co-ordinated crisis response teams in Inuit and Aboriginal communities are at least 50 percent Inuit or Aboriginal and include appropriate community members and professionals such as elders, social workers, teachers, nurses, community health representatives and victims' advocates.

Research and Evaluation

S.44 Conduct and/or sponsor qualitative, quantitative and evaluative research on violence against women in collaboration with front-line workers and other community groups directly linked with the delivery of support services to women survivors of violence.

Details

Specific topics would include:

- *the distinct forms of violence and its prevalence among different groups of women;*

- *factors identified by survivors in stopping violence in relationships;*

- *the outcome of various community practices and strategies employed to deal with woman abuse; and*

- *the effectiveness of support groups for men, including program and external factors which affect program outcomes.*

- *research findings must be made public.*

Education/Promotional Activities

S.45 Use a feminist perspective based on gender, race and class to describe the nature of all forms of violence against women in all materials and documentation related to violence against women.

S.46 Use non-print media such as audio tapes and broadcast through Aboriginal and Inuit radio and television to reach both Aboriginal and Inuit women.

Provincial-territorial Ministries of health.

Priority Setting/Allocation of Resources

S.47 Recognize institutional medical services, community-sponsored and governed services, self-help groups and health promotion programs including violence prevention programs as health care services.

S.48 Recognize and support traditional healing services as legitimate forms of healing for Aboriginal and Inuit women. This would include suicide support groups, holistic family healing, an enhanced role for elders and guidance and participation by Aboriginal and Inuit women's advocacy groups.

S.49 Implement contract compliance in funding of institutions and agencies such as hospitals and community health agencies.

Details

Conditions could include the adoption of a zero tolerance policy and a commitment to participate in a community-based and co-ordinated response to violence against women.

Human Resource Management

S.50 Use front-line workers and health care providers in the development of health service delivery protocols.

S.51 Ensure that Aboriginal peoples and Inuit have access to a full range of training opportunities to meet the self-identified needs for community-based healing and treatment programs for victims of violence.

Legislation/Regulation/Policy

S.52 Revise all health policies to recognize the complexity of violence against women and the fact that violence is not an illness.

Programs/Services/Practices

S.53 Recognize and promote the use of a feminist intervention approach with the appropriate use of medical and psychiatric services.

S.54 Establish "healing centres" on a pilot project basis to provide a safe and supportive environment for women who are in crisis as a result of violence.

Details

These centres could be long-term residential centres that provide alternative services such as crisis intervention and referral services to current medical and psychiatric models of service delivery.

S.55 Establish registries of feminist therapists from which women can choose their own therapist.

S.56 Provide client advocates in all health facilities.

S.57 Increase the level of services in Aboriginal and Inuit communities to treat alcohol, drug and solvent abuse.

Details

These services must have the appropriate professional expertise to deal with the underlying issues of violence and must promote an holistic approach.

S.58 Ensure that Aboriginal and Inuit women seeking or receiving treatment outside of their communities have access to follow-up counselling and other services once they return to their communities.

S.59 Ensure that long-term care for victims/survivors/offenders in Inuit and Aborigonal communities is designed and delivered by Inuit and Aboriginal people. It must address the root causes of violence in addition to symptomatic behaviours such as addictions. The community must be able to determine the service delivery models.

S.60 Disseminate information on the availability of government programs to community health service providers, in the language appropriate to the community.

S.61 Integrate the issue of violence prevention into health promotion programs.

Co-ordination

S.62 Recognize and encourage health practitioners to network and co-operate with front-line workers and community service workers and to participate in interagency committees on violence against women or other community co-ordinating mechanisms.

Research and Evaluation

S.63 Conduct and/or sponsor qualitative, quantitative and evaluative research on violence against women.

Details

Specific topics would include:

- *the costs of violence to the health care system including costs associated with misdiagnosis and missed diagnosis, and the total amount of human resources involved;*

- *the links between experiencing violence and various conditions suffered by women, such as depression, anorexia and bulimia;*

- *the identification of the psychological consequences of torture and the development of effective treatment programs for torture victims and their families; and*

- *the specific needs of Aboriginal women with disabilities and of Aboriginal elderly women.*

Education/Promotional Activities

S.64 Use a feminist perspective based on gender, race and class to describe the nature of all forms of violence against women in all materials and documentation related to violence against women.

S.65 Use non-print media, such as audio tapes and broadcast through Aboriginal and Inuit radio and television, to reach both Aboriginal and Inuit women.

Federal department responsible for health

Legislation/Regulation/Policy

S.66 Undertake, in co-operation with the provinces and territories, an assessment of the capabilities, the scope and the use of provisions of current funding mechanisms such as the *Canada Assistance Plan* and the *Canada Health Act*, in responding to the needs of women survivors of violence.

Programs/Services/Practices

S.67 Guarantee that all Aboriginal and Inuit women receive the same standard and quality of services as women in non-Aboriginal and non-Inuit communities.

Details

This can be achieved by having community members identify their community's needs and by ensuring that services are developed and delivered by Aboriginal people.

S.68 Increase the level of services in Aboriginal and Inuit communities to treat alcohol, drug and solvent abuse.

Details

These services must have the appropriate professional expertise to deal with the underlying issues of violence and must promote an holistic approach to violence in Aboriginal and Inuit communities.

S.69 Support the establishment of a network of healing centres to incorporate addictions and other services.

LEGAL SECTOR

Introduction

At present, the legal system does not bring much justice to women in Canada. Increasingly, it has become a series of formalized processes relying on technicalities and tactics where priority is given to following rules and precedent instead of attempting to assure that justice is achieved. As exercises in truth seeking, legal practices fall woefully short of any acceptable standard. In this action plan, solutions are put forward to be addressed by the following key participants:

- police forces

- boards and commissions

- courts and tribunals

- law schools

- voluntary legal associations

- law societies

- federal, provincial-territorial governments.

Key Problems

Justice for women in Canada has always been elusive. It was men who sat at the table writing the laws and then administering them, protecting their interests in property and safety in the process. All the rules and the evidentiary processes for determining guilt or innocence were determined from the male perspective. This exclusion from the formulation, administration, application and interpretation of the law diminished women's access to justice. It also resulted in their being harmed rather than helped by much of their contact with the system.

As the legal systems evolved, a series of safeguards were incorporated to try to balance power between the accused and the state. These safeguards have become known as the fair trial rights of the accused.

There was no obligation to consider the impact of these provisions or any other aspect of legal practice on the victims of the crime until the introduction in 1985 of the *Canadian Charter of Rights and Freedoms* equality section which supports the right to equal benefit and protection of the law for all victims as well as the accused. Even with that obligation in place, little has been done to bring a fair balance to the system. There has, however, been a clear articulation by the Supreme Court of Canada on the nature of the equality that must be achieved. In stressing the equality of outcome and therefore the importance of different treatment to reach that goal, the Supreme Court provides the framework for the large-scale initiatives and changes that are needed.

The limited criminalization of the violence committed against women is a great violation of their basic human rights to equal benefit and protection of the law, to security of the person and sometimes to life. Denial of the existence of violence is reinforced when acquittals result because of a technicality due to the process and not related to the guilt or innocence of the accused. It also comes with trivial sentences that in themselves deny the seriousness of what occurred. When crimes are inadequately defined or ignored in law, some men are given immunity from prosecution while their victims are either denied access to the courts altogether or are filtered out of the legal system in the early stages.

When the knowledge of judges is tainted by bias and myths and is marked by an absence of relevant and complete information on crimes of violence against women, the resulting adjudication cannot be fair. The rights to life and to security of the person have been severely jeopardized for women when judges have not understood the severity of the crimes of sexual assault, assault of women in intimate relationships, and threatening behaviours leading to the murder of women.

Women's lives are diminished and limited and their inequality reinforced by the violence perpetrated against them and by the fear of the next violence.

Children's safety in Canada has also been significantly jeopardized by a legal system that does not effectively deal with crimes of violence against children.

In the past, the lack of knowledge and understanding of crimes of violence against women and against children and the biases related to gender, race and class held by those administering the law were not recognized to exist at all and certainly were not deemed important enough to require remedial interventions. Legal practitioners and adjudicators were not held accountable for their behaviour and for their contributions to the violation of women's and children's equality and security. Only very recently has there been some recognition that specialized knowledge is necessary for the adjudication of these crimes. The civil process shares many of the same limitations. Although feminist legal theorists have been detailing the problems for a number of years, the legal community is now scrutinizing the legal system for bias for the first time.

The laws created, the determinations of innocence or guilt, the treatment of women victim witnesses, sentencing practices and release decisions for offenders are some of the practices which, imbued with bias, have had a negative impact on the basic human rights of women.

The legal system must undergo considerable systemic change. Some changes, such as the judicial education programs on gender equality, are being introduced but in a limited and leisurely fashion.

To the extent to which women do not receive equal benefit of the law, their basic human rights are being violated, and the equality provisions of the *Canadian Charter of Rights and Freedoms* have been offended. Laws and practices which contribute to the subordination of women are unconstitutional. There is, therefore, considerable urgency to change them.

New Orientations for the Legal Sector

L.1 **In the legal system, the tolerance of violence as it exists in unfair laws, the bias of adjudicators, and other discriminatory practices related to the administration of justice have produced significant violations of women's basic human rights. Consequently, the adoption of zero tolerance is the major new orientation for this sector.**

L.2 **The change in the criteria for appointment of police commissioners, judges and other adjudicators to give priority to those with a demonstrated understanding of equality issues and the complex dynamics of violence against women would produce a fundamental shift in the legal system that is or will be necessary to achieve justice for women.**

L.3 **Implement the equality provisions of the *Canadian Charter of Rights and Freedoms* fully for women victims and women offenders.**

L.4 **Introduce a new fundamental principle of justice that protects the right of everyone to have a response from the legal system that is free of gender, race and class bias.**

L.5 **Account fully to women for their equality and safety. This should be done by all organizations in the legal sector.**

Zero Tolerance Actions for All Organizations in the Legal Sector

Priority Setting/Allocation of Resources

L.6   Commit publicly to eradicating existing gender, race and class bias in the legal system and to fully supporting women's and children's Charter rights.

Human Resource Management

L.7   Provide training on the role of the legal system in promoting women's equality. Issues to be included in the training would deal with the unacceptable tolerance of violence in the legal system; how implementing women's rights to equality and security will change current legal practices; constitutional issues affecting women; strategies that promote the equality of women and children in the legal system; recognizing dangerous offenders; assessing the volatility of situations involving abuse and recognizing threats to women's safety; and recognizing racism including that which is directed at Aboriginal and Inuit peoples.

L.8   Evaluate the extent to which there has been an incorporation of cross cultural and gender specific knowledge provided in training, into policy formulation and practice.

Education/Promotional Activities

L.9   Initiate, with equality-seeking organizations, education programs that emphasize equality and access to justice and are designed for members to help highlight the current inequities within the legal system.

L.10   Create and disseminate to the public, in as many languages as possible, education materials that acknowledge and explain the problems of inequality and the lack of safety for women within the current legal system. Explain the changes that implementation of zero tolerance will bring.

Zero Tolerance Actions for Specific Organizations

All police forces, boards and commissions.

Human Resource Management

L.11   Recruit Aboriginal women, women of diverse cultures and those who demonstrate knowledge and an understanding of issues of sexism and racism.

L.12   Differentiate between the appropriate use and abuse of power in all policies affecting staffing practices and in the review of officers.

L.13   Provide training for all members of the force. It should teach force members how to determine the risk of further harm posed by offenders, according to research and prior patterns of abuse; explain evidentiary and safety issues related to stalking and criminal harassment, children who witness violence, disabled persons who are abused, ritual and cult abuse, date rape, sexual abuse involving breach of trust, and the use of pornography or other sexually violent media in the perpetration of abuse.

L.14 Provide cross-cultural information and training from members of Aboriginal and Inuit cultures and other cultures to improve police responses to women from different cultures and to underline the unacceptability of violence in any culture.

L.15 Provide counselling or employee assistance programs to help officers cope with the stress of their jobs in non-violent ways.

Legislation/Regulation/Policy

L.16 Create and enforce the implementation of policies to ensure that initial police response, decisions on arrest, detention and terms of any release support the safety of the victims and prevent their revictimization. For example, work to provide a maximum response time of 30 minutes in northern, remote and rural communities.

L.17 Ensure that police force policies clearly reflect the priority given to the safety of people over the protection of property.

L.18 Enforce policies dealing with officers who abuse women. They must be identified as unfit to serve in law enforcement and must experience the full consequences of the law.

Programs/Services/Practices

L.19 Create specialized units to deal with sexual assault by strangers and acquaintances, woman abuse and all crimes of harassment and assault against women and children.

L.20 Initiate programs to remove the abuser from the home whenever possible and use technology, such as alarms for women and electronic monitoring devices for the abuser, to support the woman's safety in her home. Strengthen the application of peace bonds and restraining orders through their quick implementation and by communicating the relevant information quickly to other law enforcement personnel. Confiscate firearms and other weapons from those charged with abuse.

L.21 Collect DNA evidence from all those accused of sex offences and create a DNA data bank to help identify serial offenders.

L.22 Review and evaluate the Rape Evidence Kit with an eye to reducing the level of intrusiveness while maintaining the standards required for collecting sound evidence.

L.23 Initiate, with women and women's organizations, safety audits of public and semi-public spaces as well as of police property.

Consultation

L.24 Involve women's organizations and women anti-violence experts in the setting of priorities for the force and in the development and implementation of training programs on women's equality and safety.

L.25 Create police-community working groups to develop ways to improve the safety of women in the community.

L.26 Encourage women's anti-violence organizations to report regularly on the local priority issues involving the police and the safety of women. Schedule these reports as part of police commission meetings. Create mechanisms to respond to those concerns, making changes where necessary. Include regular reports from the commission back to the organizations.

L.27 Create a women's safety advisory board locally and nationally in the **RCMP** with representation from Aboriginal and Inuit women and from women representing the diversity of women in Canada.

Co-ordination

L.28 Create protocols with community organizations to co-ordinate responses for the treatment of women and children who are victims of sexual assault and other crimes of violence. Develop crime prevention initiatives with women's organizations and other community stakeholders working against violence.

L.29 Provide or co-ordinate, with community agencies, supports for victims with disabilities. These could include **TDD** lines, signers, bliss board interpreters, information in braille and cultural interpreters with knowledge of issues of violence. Ensure the co-ordination and efficient dissemination of information affecting public safety through police computer networks (**CPIC**), timely reports to the media and other practices.

Research and Evaluation

L.30 Create mechanisms to ensure the ongoing review of police service delivery involving crimes of violence from the victims' perspective. Evaluate levels of support for victims' safety and the effectiveness of the investigation processes. Use current data-tracking projects or develop new ones to review length of time and disposition for these cases. Use results as a basis for policy revisions.

Education/Promotional Activities

L.31 Work with school personnel and with women's organizations to develop violence prevention programs for schools and for the general public. Actively support crime prevention initiatives by other community organizations where priority is given to women's and children's safety.

Accountability

L.32 Publicize the complaints process by providing easy-to-understand information in a variety of languages. Ensure that the complainant is supported during the process, and do whatever else is necessary to create an accessible, fair complaints process.

L.33 Ensure the police commissions work in a transparent manner and stay accountable to women in the community on the work done to support their safety by reporting regularly on activities.

All chief justices, judicial councils, judges and other adjudicators.

Human Resource Management

L.34 Create through the judicial councils standards of practice and behaviour that promote equality.

L.35 Develop training programs that are mandatory for judges and other adjudicators including parole board members.

Details:

The training should include:

- *recognition of gender, race and class bias;*

- *sexual abuse of power and trust;*

- *the nature of self defence for abused women;*

- *a formula for determining the risk posed by an accused;*

- *the efficacy of current treatment programs for sexual abusers and other woman abusers and realistic prospects for rehabilitation;*

- *the assessment of the expertise of experts and the value of expert testimony;*

- *the understanding of the parallels between torture and woman abuse and the understanding of the dynamics and the impact of woman abuse, including psychological and emotional abuse, and harassment.*

Legislation/Regulation/Policy

L.36 Support the safety, security and equality interests of women by enforcing legislation through the actions of the court. Ensure that sentencing reflects the severity of the crimes of woman abuse and that the harm and danger posed by sexual offenders are recognized by using the full range of sentencing allowed. Other decisions taken in the court must reflect a clear appreciation of the harms caused by the abusive behaviours perpetrated against women, especially those where there is no obvious physical injury (e.g., stalking and criminal harassment) or where there is sexual abuse by a person in a position of power or trust and the risk of harm posed by the accused. Support the security interests of children by clearly recognizing the harms of sexual and physical abuse, the psychological impact on children who witness abuse in their home and the risk of reoffending from many sexual abusers.

L.37 Ensure that policies governing conditional release practices make the safety of women and children a priority.

Programs/Services/Practices

L.38 Support the development of specialized courts or court space dedicated to the needs of children and to deal with crimes of woman abuse.

L.39 Replace preliminary hearings, wherever possible, with paper disclosure.

L.40 Make public safety interests the prime consideration in using incarceration in sentencing.

Consultation

L.41 Ensure the perspective of the victim is well represented through victim impact statements, victims' advocates, and frequent consultations on victims' issues.

L.42 Define "dangerousness" of abusers with input from women on the definition.

L.43 Develop protocols for court practices based on the *Canadian Charter of Rights and Freedoms* with input from victims.

L.44 Consult on alternatives to incarceration for crimes that do not threaten public safety.

Co-ordination

L.45 Take a leadership role in the use of the socio-legal approach to sentencing that includes treatment and post-incarceration supervision and relapse prevention treatment for abusers. Gather and integrate information and analysis from groups concerned with equality and anti-violence.

L.46 Support co-ordination between courts and victim services.

Physical Environment

L.47 Provide assistance to women to audit courthouses or locations where courts are sitting in isolated communities, and to ensure the victims do not have to have contact with those accused of crimes against them.

Accountability

L.48 Develop judicial standards of practice and behaviour for judges and justices of the peace that will promote justice and equality, and support the safety of women and of children.

L.49 Improve public access to the complaints process by publicizing the procedures and how to use them. Make proceedings of discipline committees and decisions more public. Provide detailed annual reporting of disciplinary actions. Assess need for a judicial council on Prince Edward Island.

All deans and faculty of law schools.

Human Resource Management

L.50 Recognize through promotion or other reward practices staff and faculty who work on equality-promoting initiatives.

Legislation/Regulation /Policy

L.51 Create policies to deal severely with abusive behaviour by faculty or students. Recognize the inappropriateness of such behaviour for a person who is or will be in a position of trust and power. Keep records of incidents of abuse and ensure that they are part of official records that are passed on to law societies.

Programs/Services/Practices

L.52 Integrate the issues of sexism, racism and class bias, the rights of victims and other equality issues under the *Canadian Charter of Rights and Freedoms* into all aspects of the curriculum. Introduce specific units on the experience of victims in the legal system, the nature and impact of crimes of violence including sexual abuse of persons with disabilities, ritual abuse and other crimes not yet well recognized.

L.53 Establish protocols for recording and passing on to law societies information on incidents of abuse and harassment by students who may apply in the future for admission to the society.

Consultation

L.54 Determine program priorities, and develop new curricula with women students, faculty and with women who are experts from outside the school on the nature of equality, issues of violence against women, the use of the *Canadian Charter of Rights and Freedoms* and the legal system.

L.55 Work with survivors of violence to bring needed change to legal theory and practice.

L.56 Develop partnerships with women and women's organizations and actively work toward solutions to problems women identify in the legal system.

Co-ordination

L.57 Develop co-operative, equality-promoting programs with women experts including violence survivors to support change in legal practice.

L.58 Co-ordinate curricula development with trainers of para-legals and other legal system workers with community colleges and other legal training institutes.

All voluntary legal associations.

Priority Setting/Allocation of Resources

L.59 Through the Canadian Bar Association Ethics Committee, undertake initiatives to promote women's equality and support women's safety. Identify ways to reduce acquittals based on "legal" technicalities and create protocols for defence counsel to reduce victim-witness harassment in sexual assault and other woman abuse cases.

Legislation/Regulation/Policy

L.60 Develop policies to articulate the specific ways the association will support the work or actions of its members who are doing equality and safety promotion work on behalf of women and children. Create models of policies and protocols on the treatment of women clients to promote the quality and safety of women and of their children. Encourage the adoption of these policies and protocols by legal firms.

Programs/Services/Practices

L.61 Create and disseminate model human resource management policies including policies on workplace harassment and training packages to address gender inequality, racism and other discriminatory attitudes and acts.

Co-ordination

L.62 Co-ordinate initiatives designed to remedy the problems women experience in the courts.

Research and Evaluation

L.63 Gather data on the impact of the legal system on women with particular focus on the harms of gender, race and class bias.

All law societies.

Priority Setting/Allocation of Resources

L.64 Initiate, immediately, a process for more effective detection of those members who abuse, including lawyers who attempt to or waive fees for sex. Removal from practice would be obligatory until rehabilitation is assured.

Human Resource Management

L.65 Ensure comprehensive training for staff and benchers on issues of violence. Place special emphasis on sexual abuse involving breach of trust and on the impact of violence and legal system responses on women who experience compounded oppression.

Legislation/Regulation/Policy

L.66 Create specific standards of practice behaviour for lawyers that will promote equality and security for women and for children.

L.67 Create admission criteria policies that are explicit from the perspective of women's and children's safety. The policies would clearly define "good character" and the type of behaviour that would be deemed abusive and thus prohibit entry into the profession.

Consultation

L.68 Consult with women experts within and outside the profession when setting program priorities, generally, and on legal issues related to equality and safety, specifically.

Co-ordination

L.69 Ensure that the most relevant feminist analysis on issues of violence and equality, including work from outside the legal system, is made available to members.

Accountability

L.70 Increase lay membership of law society complaint and discipline committees. Appoint those with demonstrated understanding of equality issues and issues of violence, especially involving breach of trust issues, and who reflect the composition of the population.

All federal, provincial and territorial governments where relevant to their jurisdiction.

Priority Setting/Allocation of Resources

L.71 Acknowledge the present inequities in the legal system. Commit to the full realization of women's and children's rights to safety, security and equality enshrined in the *Canadian Charter of Rights and Freedoms*.

Legislation/Regulation/Policy

L.72 Review and evaluate, with women's organizations, legislative changes dealing with psychological or emotional abuse.

L.73 Amend or create new statutes where necessary to support women's equality and security interests through legislation and regulation in the following areas:

- *Criminal Code* — repeal soliciting provisions; change obscenity provisions to reflect the prohibition of sexually violent and degrading material, and add "sex" and remove "wilfully" to hate law sections.

- Recognize more clearly and explicitly in law the serious threat to security of the person and the gender-specific nature of most crimes of stalking or criminal harassment as well as the negative cumulative effects of the acts involved where the whole is much greater than the parts.

- Extend publication bans for sexual assault victims to the pretrial and other adjudicative processes.

- Recognize sexual abuse involving breach of trust as a specific crime of sexual assault.

- *Correction and Conditional Release Act* — ensure that the definition of serious harm includes emotional or psychological harm of sexual assault for women as well as for children.

- *Federal Immigration and Refugee Act* — recognize women fleeing gender persecution as refugees.

- *Provincial Crimes Compensation Acts* — extend provisions to increase the amount of compensation for victims including those of institutional abuse and to amend any time limitation in statute that would discriminate against adult survivors of incest receiving compensation.

- Civil remedies for women who are sexually exploited or abused in the consumption of pornography, by health practitioners, counsellors or therapists.

L.74 Amend human rights legislation to increase compensation for victims.

L.75 Review and amend, with consultation, the following legislation to protect children's security interests:

- child welfare legislation — to define children who witness violence as children in need of protection.

- *Divorce Act* and all legislation dealing with custody and access — violence by one spouse against another is explicitly deemed to be relevant in determining custody.

L.76 Develop clear legislation on zero tolerance requirements for self-regulating
professions concerning sexual abuse
that includes, at a minimum:

- offences and penalties for sexual
  violation and abuse defined by
  seriousness into several levels;

- prohibitions on practice during any
  process of appeal after a finding of
  guilt of sexual misconduct;

- prohibitions on any automatic rein-
  statement to the profession after
  revocation of licence with onus on
  the offender to prove there is no
  longer a safety risk;

- the requirement for each self-
  regulatory body to establish a
  sexual abuse prevention and monitoring committee to work with
  government to oversee the development and implementation of effective and accessible mechanisms for
  the reporting of sexual abuse;

- the realignment of discipline hearings to ensure the fuller participation of complainants, public interest
  intervenors and experts whose
  interventions, will promote or
  uphold the safety of the public with
  testimony on issues such as the
  dynamics and harms of sexual abuse
  involving a breach of trust, the risk
  of harm from the abuser to other
  members of the public and the
  statistical probability data that the
  abuser will abuse again.

L.77 Enact policies to prohibit the use of
pornography and sexually degrading
material by sex offenders serving in any
correctional institution on the grounds
that it will weaken the effects of any
counselling program.

Programs/Services/Practices

L.78 Create special courts for crimes of
violence. Judges, Crown attorneys and
clerks working in these specialized
courts would be appointed for their
knowledge or aptitude to acquire
knowledge on the full range of issues of
violent crimes against women and
children.

L.79 Designate senior Crown attorneys who
have been provided with specialized
training to handle dangerous offender
applications, sexual abuse involving
breach of trust, ritual abuse and other
cases where the victims are disadvantaged because evidentiary issues are
currently not well understood.

L.80 Reinstate an expanded Court
Challenges Program.

L.81 Expand legal aid, victim support and
women's advocacy programs, including
pilot projects for women with disabilities and other victim witnesses who
have special needs in the courtroom,
until equal access for all women is
achieved.

L.82 Train legal aid lawyers to deal with
woman abuse.

L.83 Create national crime prevention initiatives that give priority to the safety of women and children. Begin with the allocation of resources for community-based violence prevention activities to shelters, rape crisis centres and other anti-violence community organizations to support a national crime prevention week/month.

L.84 Appoint a national co-ordinator for the management of sex offenders. This individual must have demonstrated understanding of the primary role that abuse of power and misogyny play in the sexual offences committed. The mandate should include the overhaul and expansion of counselling programs to recognize the element of accountability to women and to the communities served by the programs.

L.85 Create a victims' advocate office and a victims' bill of rights.

L.86 Ensure any new Aboriginal system(s) of justice are developed and administered with the full participation of Aboriginal women.

L.87 Create policies that can be used as models for hiring, performance review and promotion in legal services within the next year and generic training programs for all legal practitioners within the next two years. Give priority for hiring and promotion in government legal practice to those with specialist knowledge of equality and violence issues. Appoint those with demonstrated understanding of equality issues as judges, parole board members, human rights commissioners, other tribunal members and all other adjudicators.

Consultation

L.88 Review laws and practices to ascertain their impact on women's safety and equality and recommend appropriate changes.

Details:

- Include women's organizations, judges, Crown attorneys, police and other legal practitioners in the review process.

- Consider practices and orders that are specifically related to:

  - issues of disclosure of personal information of victim-witnesses in preliminary hearings, cross examinations and through subpoenas;

  - sexual assault by acquaintances and persons in positions of trust;

  - sentencing guidelines that reflect the severity of crimes of woman abuse;

  - evidentiary issues regarding sexual abuse of women with disabilities;

  - ritual abuse;

  - abuse of women involving pornography;

  - issues of racism;

  - abuse of domestic workers and the experience of immigrant women in the legal system;

  - practices related to circuit courts in the North and isolated communities; and

  - the review of gun control.

L.89 Develop community justice and policing initiatives with the full participation of Aboriginal and Inuit women. The women must be involved in determining appropriate sanctions for all cases of violence against women and children which may include counselling at outpost camps or community facilities administered by elders and/or counselling while incarcerated in a correctional facility.

Co-ordination

L.90 Support the co-ordination of courts and counselling programs for a more effective socio-judicial approach to sentencing by developing a framework with policies and guidelines for evaluation.

L.91 Co-ordinate a review of the status of women incarcerated for killing their abusers with the Elizabeth Fry Society and co-ordinate a review with a pardon/release process where possible.

L.92 Establish crisis response teams in all Aboriginal and Inuit communities, with membership of experts and lay persons identified by the community, to co-ordinate assessment, response, intervention and referral procedures.

Research and Evaluation

L.93 Provide funds to monitor sentencing and other judicial decision-making practices by individuals with a clear understanding of the equality issues for victims and the issues of violence from a feminist perspective.

L.94 Create equality and justice monitoring, evaluation and advocacy centres to bring Charter-based equality analysis to legal data and practices.

L.95 Monitor plea bargaining practices in crimes of violence with priority given to the murder of women, woman assault and sexual assault cases.

L.96 Initiate research projects on the costs associated with offending and re-offending.

Accountability

L.97 Amend police Acts to create civilian police complaints commissions with the specific articulated purpose of upholding the safety of women and children as well as general public safety interests.

L.98 Appoint those with specialist knowledge of sexual abuse involving breach of trust to the commissions for the adjudication of complaints of sexual offences committed by police officers. Create special sub-committees of specialists to hear those complaints or provide intensive training on the issue to the members themselves.

L.99 Increase significantly the lay membership of all judicial councils and Justices of the peace review councils. Appoint those who demonstrate knowledge of legal equity issues, who bring gender equity to the council and reflect the composition of the population.

L.100 Expand powers of councils to provide a range of sanctions for behaviour violations. These could include reprimand, temporary suspensions for education, discipline and treatment or recommendations for permanent removal.

L.101 Expand powers of the councils to review judicial decisions given by other bodies, such as discipline tribunals, that overturn decisions or lighten penalties where women's safety might be affected.

L.102 Amend coroners' acts and create other legislation to compel inquests to be held after each murder of a woman to determine how the death might have been prevented and what changes might be made so other women's lives might be saved. The amendments would provide for representation by women's anti-violence or legal advocacy organizations to ensure that a victims' advocate is present and would give the coroner or designated others the responsibility for the implementation of the resulting recommendations.

L.103 Review legal system practices and legislation, regulations, policies, procedures and guidelines against the standards provided in the *Canadian Charter of Rights and Freedoms*, to find ways to remedy problem areas and ensure that victims receive the equal benefit and protection of the law and security of the person as provided in the Charter.

L.104 Report annually on progress made in implementing recommendations regarding justice initiatives made in the jurisdiction by task forces, commissions and advisors in the past five years.

WORKPLACE SECTOR

Introduction

Working for pay has become increasingly important in the lives of women in Canada. However, for many women, the workplace reinforces experiences of inequality and unequal power relations based on gender, race and class. Women are undervalued, underpaid, sexually harassed and assaulted.

Specifically, the following key participants have been identified:

- Employers (public and private sectors)

- Unions and professional associations

- Federal-provincial/territorial mechanisms (human rights commissions, ministries of labour, workers' compensation agencies, labour relations boards etc.).

Key Problems:

While socio-economic reforms, policies and practices to promote social and economic equality for women continue to be implemented, key problems do persist in terms of the safety and security of women in the workplace.

- Violence and harassment are not acknowledged as valid workplace problems nor addressed in a systematic and collaborative manner by managers and unions.

- Workplace violence and harassment are not understood as part of the wider context of violence against women, gender power relations, and race and class inequalities.

- The relationship between the ability to perform and the presence of safe working conditions is not recognized.

New Orientations for the Workplace Sector

WP.1 Eliminating violence against women in the workplace must be part of an overall strategy that addresses the economic inequality experienced by women.

WP.2 Work values must change. Such principles as co-operation, sharing and consensus building must be perceived as equal in value to control and competition.

Zero Tolerance Actions for All Organizations and Individuals in the Workplace Sector

Priority Setting/Allocation of Resources

WP.3 Subscribe to a policy of zero tolerance that supports women's safety, security and equality based on:

- equal access to all resources and programs;

- equal value for women's experience in all employment policies, practices, programs and services; and

- an accurate reflection of women's needs in all employment and related activities.

Accountability

WP.4 In collaboration with unions, employers must develop and implement a written code of conduct based on the Zero Tolerance Policy which promotes equality and guarantees safety and security for all workers, employees and clients.

Details:

Adherence to the code must be ensured through:

- *the adoption of a comprehensive strategy for educating workers, employees and clients about the philosophical background, the values and the principles inherent in the code;*

- *performance reviews with strong sanctions (i.e., warning, missed opportunity for a promotion, dismissal) for violating the code; and*

- *effective complaint procedures.*

Local women's organizations with expertise in this area must be involved to this undertaking.

Zero Tolerance Actions for Specific Organizations

> **All employers, unions and professional associations from both the public and private sectors working together.**

Legislation/Regulation/Policy

WP.5 Develop and implement a policy on violence in the workplace, including sexual harassment, as recommended in the Zero Tolerance Policy.

WP.6 Establish, amend or support policies for workers/employees regarding absences and poor performance caused by violence against women.

WP.7 Demonstrate a firm commitment to ending violence in the workplace in any negotiations.

Details

From a union's perspective, this could include:

- *bargaining for strong no-harassment provisions in collective agreements and contract language that deals with safe work environments and the issue of abuse;*

- *extending equal protection through anti-discrimination clauses and support to members who are lesbians, women of colour, immigrant women, women with disabilities and older women; and*

- *adopting policies that discourage/prohibit all sexist and racist practices in union functions.*

Programs/Services/Practices

WP.8 Conduct safety audits and violence prevention programs.

Education/Promotional Activities

WP.9 Educate non-traditional workplaces about the subtle forms of violence, such as the lack of integration of women workers/employees in the workplace or the isolation of women workers/employees because of their small numbers.

All federal-provincial/territorial mechanisms (human rights commissions, ministries of labour, worker's compensation agencies, labour relations boards etc.).

Legislation/Regulation/Policy

WP.10 Legally mandate policies on sexual harassment and on discrimination based on gender and race and make available resources for training and education in line with human rights codes. (Sexual harassment policies must include gender harassment. It can undermine the work atmosphere and is as harmful as the more commonly known sexual harassment).

WP.11 Ensure that labour relations laws are amended to include harassment in health and safety regulations.

WP.12 Recognize unsafe working conditions due to sexual harassment as a valid health and safety concern and compensate accordingly (including counselling costs) under workers' compensation regulations.

WP.13 Recognize post-traumatic stress disorder as a form of injury that can result from sexual harassment in the workplace.

WP.14 Ensure that winning compensation for sexual harassment under human rights acts does not prevent complainants from accessing other compensation for victims of crime as provided in federal, provincial or territorial legislation.

Research and Evaluation

WP.15 Evaluate sexual harassment policies and regulations adopted by private and public entities.

Details:

Such an evaluation must include:

- *the handling of complaints including decisions and dispositions of cases by judicial, quasi-judicial and administrative tribunals; and*

- *the incidence of sexual harassment of women from specific groups such as Aboriginal women, immigrant women, women of colour, women from other ethnic groups, women with disabilities, older women and lesbians.*

The Zero Tolerance Policy is to be used as a standard for evaluation.

MILITARY SECTOR

Introduction

A large public employer in Canada, the Canadian Forces has military bases throughout the country that are adjacent to or integrated into civilian communities where they have considerable impact. Many women live under the influence of military policy and procedures, specifically women members of the forces and spouses of military men.

Key Problems:

- The doctrine, culture and hierarchical structures of the Canadian Forces create an atmosphere where violence against women is fostered and tolerated.

- Spouses of military men are vulnerable physically, psychologically and financially. They are transferred frequently, often isolated and deprived of established support systems of extended family and long-time friends. The man's military career is seen as primary, and frequent changes of location make career progression very difficult for spouses. As a result, they are often dependent on husbands and on the Department of National Defence.

- The chain of command often ignores violence against women committed by military husbands. Command does not want to deal with the problems. Discipline for violence would disrupt the military career of the man and could also affect the cohesion of his unit. Women are afraid of the career consequences for their husbands if they report violence.

- Military men who resent working with women often harass women co-workers by making sexist comments and collective, sustained, serious verbal aggression designed to destroy the confidence of the women.

- Pornography is tolerated and openly displayed on bases and in training schools.

- Even though Canadian Forces policy prohibits discrimination against lesbians, the rejection of and the verbal and physical abuse of lesbians and gay men is a reality of military life.

New Orientations for the Military Sector

MI.1 **The Department of National Defence must commit to equality for women and include women, both military members and spouses, in all decisions that affect their lives.**

MI.2 **Training of men for combat and authoritarian military structures can make men very aggressive and domineering. This must be acknowledged by the Department and the chain of command. The Department must counterbalance combat readiness with human relations training that emphasizes the inappropriateness and danger of aggression in interpersonal relationships.**

MI.3 **Leaders of the Canadian Forces and base commanders must question the male-dominated hierarchical culture of the forces and determine to what degree maintenance of that culture is necessary for effective operations. The system should be significantly altered to give military personnel and their spouses more control over their lives.**

Zero Tolerance Actions for the Military Sector

The Department of National Defence

Priority Setting/Allocation of Resources

MI.4   Establish the zero tolerance committee called for in the policy and ensure that membership is drawn from senior ranking officers, military women and spouses of military members including representatives of the Organization of Spouses of Military Members (OSOMM).

MI.5   Strengthen the policies prohibiting sexism, racism and discrimination against lesbians and gay men and enforce policies vigorously and evenly throughout all ranks.

MI.6   Ensure that military women and the spouses of military men who live in violent situations have quick access to support services and can leave any situation of violence, regardless of where the base is located, in Canada or abroad.

MI.7   Increase resources to Family Resource Centres and clarify their mandate to include operation outside the base chain of command. Centres must maintain links with each other and work closely with zero tolerance committees.

Human Resource Management

MI.8   Increase the presence of military women throughout the administrative hierarchy of military bases at all decision-making levels.

MI.9   Adopt the objective of having 10 percent of senior officer positions filled by women, who represent the diversity of women in the Canadian population, within three years.

MI.10   Identify systemic barriers to women's participation. For example, ensure that the physical ability test does not exceed the standard required to do the job. Test women against this standard and not in competition with men.

MI.11   Make all military members and civilian staff aware of what constitutes a poisoned work environment for women and what constitutes sexual harassment. Emphasize the seriousness and consequences of breaching policies.

MI.12   Have the zero tolerance committee review every allegation of gender or sexual harassment and recommend appropriate solutions.

MI.13   Establish a telephone contact with the Department of National Defence, outside the chain of command, to facilitate reporting of harassment and assault when the woman cannot come forward for fear of repercussions.

MI.14   Keep records of all harassment cases to document the dimensions of the problem and to assist in eradicating violence against women in the ranks.

MI.15   Establish support groups to help women cope with integration into a male-dominated workplace.

MI.16   Establish a fair policy for employing civilian spouses of military members.

MI.17 Facilitate women's choice of physicians (both military members and spouses) and, where distance is a factor, provide transportation for those who would like to consult a civilian physician off the base.

Legislation/Regulation/Policy

MI.18 Have the zero tolerance committee review all policies and practices that govern the lives of military spouses and develop an action plan to implement required changes.

MI.19 Implement a protocol requiring all military personnel to:

- refrain from persuading either women spouses or military women to withdraw their complaints against male members;

- recognize that women are under pressure not to report violence;

- recognize that violence against women causes serious harm; and

- respect accommodation choices of military women and military wives, on or off base, and ensure that accommodation respects the right to privacy.

MI.20 Provide safe, accessible, affordable child care for all children of military personnel, recognizing the equal right of women spouses to use child care.

MI.21 Require strict confidentiality for all counselling and medical records with release only to authorized counselling and medical staff and not to senior ranking officers.

MI.22 Facilitate swift access for women to civilian police officers, Crown attorneys and legal services off the base, as well as to shelters and all services in the surrounding communities, even if these decisions involve air transportation.

MI.23 Prohibit the display on base premises of materials that are pornographic and degrading to women; no public funds may be used to purchase films, violent videos or any other pornographic material.

Co-ordination

MI.24 Establish links between women's services on the military base and those in neighbouring communities.

Education/Promotional Activities

MI.25 Develop an awareness program to eliminate sexism, racism and homophobia designed and delivered by feminist service providers, military women and spouses of military men, and include:

- information on all forms of violence including economic abuse;

- videos, lectures, brochures and posters addressed to military men of all ranks, presenting methods of intervention for those in positions of command and responsibility;

- knowledge of the extent and dynamics of violence;

- the repercussions of violent acts on women's health and their career development; and

- the repercussions of abusive acts on social and military life on bases.

Accountability

MI.26 Report annually to Parliament through the Minister of National Defence on progress made in the following areas:

- numbers of women members within the military including occupation, rank and self-identified race;

- cases of sexual and racial harassment dealt with and their outcome;

- cases of discrimination against lesbians and gay men and their outcome.

- policy changes made to benefit spouses of military men and an evaluation of their impact; and

- resources provided to Family Resource Centres and the programs and services offered.

Family Resource Centres

Priority Setting/Allocation of Resources

MI.27 Subscribe to a client-centred model of service delivery.

MI.28 Create a community board to establish priorities and directions for activities. Membership should be democratically drawn from among military spouses and military women.

Programs/Services/Practices

MI.29 Distribute information on issues of violence, family planning and the sharing of family responsibilities.

MI.30 Arrange for training in languages generally used on the base and in the surrounding community for women who are isolated due to language barriers.

MI.31 Advocate on behalf of women who are having difficulties with the military or with service deliverers.

MI.32 Keep up-to-date information on women's resources in the civilian community and make appropriate referrals.

MI.33 Undertake a safety audit of military bases and press for the necessary modifications to ensure that each base takes action to improve women's safety. Check lighting, lanes, remote areas and recreational sites, etc.

Accountability

MI.34 Report on activities and progress annually to the general population of women on the base.

EDUCATION SECTOR

Introduction

Schools, colleges and universities significantly contribute to the social, psychological and physical development as well as to the cognitive skills of students. Students are highly influenced and shaped by the structure of the system, by curriculum content, by attitudes and behaviours of educators, by learning methods, by peer relationships and by overall institutional environments. All personnel within educational institutions must be seen and must see themselves as being in positions of trust with students.

Schools have an authoritarian structure giving educators and other staff a great deal of power relative to students. Such power dynamics undermine self-protection messages that tell students they have a right to say no on one hand, yet must bow to adult authority on the other. While it is necessary to regulate behaviour in educational institutions this must be achieved through more co-operative power sharing.

The educational system alone cannot be charged with changing society's attitudes toward women and eliminating violence. However, alongside the family and the media, educational institutions have the greatest opportunity to play a positive role in change. Working toward equality for women and zero tolerance of violence among the youth of Canada will have far-reaching effects in reducing violence against women.

The enormous demands on educational resources are recognized. However, as our consultations revealed, people in Canada clearly believe the education system has an important role to play in ending violence and promoting equality. Many feel that requisite changes could be accommodated by altering current materials and courses and by equipping educators to deliver the altered content in a manner that demonstrates equality and non-violence. This will require realignment of resources and priorities to emphasize the goals of equality and

non-violence. A commitment by ministries of education, ministries of colleges and universities, boards of education, educational institutions (schools, colleges and universities), teachers' federations, voluntary bodies such as parent-teacher organizations, parent volunteers and the students themselves is essential.

Currently, the educational system is being challenged to adapt to world competitiveness standards. Any moves in that direction must incorporate the needs of women both in terms of equality and safety. Failure to do so will seriously compound existing problems and result in even greater disparities between women and men in the work force and in the sharing of Canada's prosperity.

Key Problems

- Violence among students and between students and teachers is a growing concern in schools, colleges and universities. The abuse is frequently based on sexism and/or racism. Often, there is an absence of clear, appropriate strategies to prevent or resolve violent situations.

- Some students who suffer violence either through assault or through witnessing violence in their own homes may become abusive themselves as playground bullies or in dating relationships. Others may manifest symptoms of being abused through low achievement, erratic behaviour or failure to participate. Often, despite symptoms, the abuse goes undetected.

- The physical and social environments of schools, colleges and universities frequently create inequality and danger for girls and women.

New Orientations for the Education Sector

ED.1   The entire education sector (provincial/territorial ministries of education, ministries of colleges and universities, Aboriginal/Inuit school authorities, boards of education, all educational institutions, including Aboriginal, Inuit and private schools, teachers' federations, voluntary bodies such as parent-teacher associations, parent volunteers and student governments) must create the strongest possible equality model based on gender, race and class.

Details

This includes the following specific actions:

- *altering all administrative structures and practices to better reflect equality and more equitable power sharing.*

- *requiring all faculty members and staff to be role models in encouraging others to share power and to be respectful regardless of student/faculty status, gender, race or class.*

- *making the building of student self-awareness and self-esteem a core value of all educational settings.*

- *creating a social culture that values interaction between boys and girls, women and men other than conventional dating relationships.*

- *teaching and requiring the practice of peaceful conflict resolution.*

- *emphasizing the rights of girls and women and the responsibilities of boys and men to respect these rights.*

- *ensuring that guidance counsellors have current information and have received instruction on the status of women in Canada, and are prepared to guide girls into the full range of careers.*

- *taking ameliorative measures to accelerate the attainment of equality in all aspects of education.*

Zero Tolerance Actions for All Organizations and Individuals in the Education Sector

Priority Setting/Allocation of Resources

ED.2   Implement violence prevention strategies that focus on violence against girls and women. Ensure that such programs are culturally relevant.

ED.3   Conduct safety audits of all educational facilities to identify places and situations that create danger for girls and women.

Human Resource Management

ED.4   Make the safety of girls and women a priority when selecting staff.

ED.5   Use employment equity strategies to equalize, in all occupations and at all levels, the proportion of women and men and the representation of the races within the community served.

ED.6   Train staff members to recognize the linkages between inequality and violence and to incorporate this knowledge into their work.

ED.7   Make awareness of inequality and its linkages to violence against women a formal rating factor in staff performance appraisals.

ED.8 Implement effective, accessible policies against sexual and racial violence and enforce them fairly.

Legislation/Regulation/Policy

ED.9 Develop culturally relevant protocols that outline actions to be taken when acts of violence occur. The protocols should give priority to the safety of victims and refer victims to appropriate women-centred and culturally relevant services.

ED.10 Implement sexual harassment policies with strong and effective redress mechanisms.

Consultation

ED.11 Consult widely with women's organizations, including women's teachers' federations, that have resources and knowledge in the areas of equality and ending violence.

Co-ordination

ED.12 Work closely with other education partners and women's groups to ensure a consistent message on equality and ending violence, and to share resources.

Zero Tolerance Actions for Specific Organizations or Individuals

All student governments at elementary, secondary and post-secondary levels.

Priority Setting/Resource Allocation

ED.13 Make girls' and women's equality and safety a priority.

ED.14 Facilitate equal participation of girls and women in all structures and activities.

Programs/Services/Practices

ED.15 Monitor the institutional administration's progress on implementing zero tolerance and assist in achieving its goals.

Accountability

ED.16 Make the student body aware of all activities aimed at achieving equality and ending violence and report annually to students on progress.

All boards of education including Aboriginal, Inuit and private schools, and all elementary and secondary schools.

Priority Setting/Allocation of Resources

ED.17 Aim at gender, race and class equality and the ending of violence as priorities. Reflect these goals in mission statements and throughout the entire strategic planning process.

ED.18 Re-align budget allocations to support implementation of the Zero Tolerance Policy.

Human Resource Management

ED.19 Recognize the positions of trust and authority held by staff in educational institutions in the selection and placement of staff.

Details

Safeguard students by:

- *evaluating sexist, racist and class attitudes at pre-employment interviews;*

- *asking at the interview and in checking references about past behaviour or complaints related to violence against girls and women; and*

- *evaluating awareness of appropriate behavioural limits with girls and women students.*

ED.20 Train staff on how to recognize symptoms of abuse and in the use of appropriate first-level intervention techniques.

ED.21 Train educators to recognize the links between gender and race inequality and violence, and to identify the full range of behaviours that constitute gender and race discrimination including the more subtle manifestations.

ED.22 Hold all educators accountable for sexist or racist behaviours they display.

ED.23 Do not hire any educator who abuses students; dismiss any educator who abuses students.

ED.24 Recognize the vulnerability of teachers to false allegations of abuse by students but avoid exaggerating the risk.

Legislation/Regulation/Policy

ED.25 Develop protocols that obligate staff members to refer student victims and student perpetrators of violence to appropriate, culturally relevant services without delay.

ED.26 Provide support, including peer support programs, for student victims and student perpetrators of violence who are undergoing counselling.

Programs/Services/Practices

ED.27 Conduct a gender-aware violence prevention program.

ED.28 Make violence prevention a part of all curricula.

ED.29 Make all programs and services (including extra-curricular and sport activities) available in an equal and appropriate fashion to all students, male and female.

ED.30 Direct particular efforts at girls in physical education and sports activities to ensure that they develop and reach their full physical potential.

ED.31 Base all educational practices and violence prevention activities on gender-aware information so girls and women derive equal benefit and protection.

ED.32 Introduce ameliorative programs, services and practices to overcome the unequal status of girls and women within society and within educational institutions.

ED.33 Implement programs that assist young mothers to stay in school.

Consultation

ED.34 Use the expertise and educational resources of women's groups in the development of policy, practices, programs and procedures and pay for these services according to scales used for other types of consultants.

Co-ordination

ED.35 Link prevention strategies and equality initiatives with wider community strategies to meet the total needs of students.

ED.36 Exchange and share knowledge and resources to ensure that all efforts within the education sector complement each other in achieving safety and equality.

Research and Evaluation

ED.37 Assess the effectiveness and success of any program, policy or practice designed to ensure girls' and women's safety and to achieve equality.

Details

The assessment should include as a minimum:

- *the differential impact on both genders;*

- *an examination of whether girls' and women's needs are being met; and*

- *an evaluation of resource use.*

Education/Promotional Activities

ED.38 Consider students' safety and equality needs in any educational activities and promotions within schools.

Accountability

ED.39 Hold all staff and students accountable for sexist and racist behaviour.

ED.40 Create clear, accessible, grievance procedures for students who are abused and ensure that students are represented on adjudicating bodies by other students or, in the case of young elementary children, by parents or children's advocates.

ED.41 Make public all policies, procedures and practices aimed at achieving equality and ending violence. This would include evaluations of progress toward those goals.

All colleges and universities.

Priority Setting/Allocation of Resources

ED.42 Make prevention of violence against women a top priority.

ED.43 Formulate and implement policies to alter the hostility toward women in the social and educational environment on campuses.

ED.44 Ensure that resource allocations equally support the activities and needs of women students.

Human Resource Management

ED.45 Accelerate employment equity programs to achieve a balance of male/female faculty more quickly.

ED.46 Train faculty on the dynamics of violence against women and its links to inequality.

ED.47 Provide support for feminist faculty members.

Legislation/Regulation/Policy

ED.48 Implement strong sexual harassment-prevention policies and protocols.

ED.49 Implement policies and protocols to deal with sexism and racism.

Programs/Services/Practices

ED.50 Make equality and the prevention of violence against women part of the course content of all faculties including professional schools such as law, medicine and social work.

ED.51 Include material on the impacts of experiencing violence on learning into the curricula of all faculties of education. It should discuss the recognition of the symptoms in a student experiencing violence, provide appropriate first-level responses to students who are suffering violence and elaborate on the links between inequality and violence.

ED.52 Ensure that diplomas and degrees granted by faculties which specialize in Aboriginal programs have equal status to the more general degrees.

ED.53 Implement an equity program that encourages girls and women to enter male-dominated fields of study. It should also support women in transforming the traditional male culture that isolates and alienates women in these fields.

ED.54 Support programs, such as women's centres, that assist women who are victims.

Co-ordination

ED.55 Link violence prevention strategies with those of the larger non-academic community.

ED.56 Use community resources and staff from shelters, rape crisis centres and women's centres to train faculty members and deliver course content on violence against women to students.

Research and Evaluation

ED.57 Work closely with service providers to decide what research is needed most urgently in the area of violence against women.

ED.58 Recognize feminist research and social action research methodology.

Accountability

ED.59 Make public all policy and program goals aimed at achieving equality and ending violence along with the annual evaluation of progress toward these goals.

> Provincial/territorial ministries of education.

Programs/Services/Practices

ED.60 Make the following changes to curricula.

(a) Make sex education compulsory and design courses that include material on:

- gender relationships and shared responsibility as well as biological facts;

- equality between women and men;

- relationships between lesbians and between gay men; and

- sexuality of persons with disabilities.

(b) Make life skills education compulsory and include content on positive parenting skills, such as non-violent discipline, and on prevention of violence against women and children.

(c) Make media literacy programs, that help "decode" media violence, sex-role stereotyping and the misleading portrayal of women, compulsory for schools at all levels.

(d) Alter core curricula to provide an equal portion of content about women in all their diversity.

(e) Have Canadian history curricula evaluated by Aboriginal and Inuit educators to ensure adequate and accurate content on the history of Aboriginal and Inuit peoples.

(f) Include the prevention of violence against women in the course content for all subjects.

(g) Make women's studies available as an option in high school.

ED.61 Designate a school within each province/territory as a pilot model school environment to achieve gender and race equality and the eradication of violence. Use the knowledge gained through the pilot school project to improve the environments of all schools.

All teachers' federations.

Legislation/Regulation/Policy

ED.62 Take a leadership role in reviewing professional codes of ethics for teachers. In the review, identify and remove potential or real barriers to disclosure of abuse by teachers and to holding teachers accountable for abuse inflicted by them.

Programs/Services/Practices

ED.63 Include content on equality of women and prevention of violence against women in all professional activities with teachers.

ED.64 Continue the work initiated by a number of women's federations on equality and violence issues.

ED.65 Provide in-service training to teachers on:

- recognizing their positions of trust/authority;

- recognizing that consent for sexual involvement with a student is not possible due to the power imbalance inherent in the teacher-student relationship; and

- how to maintain warm, nurturing relationships with students within safe touching boundaries.

Consultation

ED.66 Build on the working relationship currently established by women's federations with women working in the anti-violence movement.

ED.67 Continue to provide expert input into government educational policies and programs on education, children and violence.

ED.68 Take part in an open dialogue with child advocacy groups on the abuse of children by teachers.

Research and Evaluation

ED.69 Undertake research that furthers the understanding of the impact on learning when a student is experiencing violence.

Education/Promotional Activities

ED.70 Solicit and publish articles on violence against children and violence in the schools in all federation publications.

ED.71 Include information on women's equality and its links to violence in all publications.

Accountability

ED.72 Report annually on work done on the prevention of violence against women and on women's equality.

MEDIA SECTOR

Introduction

The media are an inordinately powerful source of ideas in Canadian life. Books, magazines, newspapers, television, videos, video games and radio bombard us with messages round the clock that shape our attitudes, often without our awareness.

Unfortunately, sexism, racism and violence feature prominently in media. Distorted and dangerous messages about women prevail; women are shown as subservient, in a limited range of roles that often portray them as sexual, worthy targets of male violence. Women's experiences are seldom the focus of news or current affairs, and their opinions are put forward less frequently than men's. Women are constantly used to sell products and are stalked, beaten, raped and mutilated in the name of entertainment.

There is a strong link between the portrayal of women in the media and the violence enacted against women in Canada every day. Women and children both describe how their abusers use pornography in the violent acts committed against them. The regulation of violence against women in the media is clearly a women's safety and child protection issue.

Key Problems

- For over a decade, the Canadian Radio-television Telecommunication Commission (CRTC) has encouraged broadcasters to self regulate the violence on television and the portrayal of women. Past efforts have not achieved the needed results. As long as self regulation continues to be ineffective and licences are renewed for broadcasters who deliver violent programs into Canadian homes, women doubt that the government is adequately supporting their safety and equality interests.

- The print media operate with almost no accountability to women or to the public generally, and press councils are not always receptive to the complaints filed by women. Violence against women is often sensationally reported and the incidents individualized. Less dramatic violence is ignored. There is little analysis of the systemic causes of violence. When violence is linked to equality, the media discussion is often adversarial. Important reports on violence against women are buried on inner pages and are sometimes juxtaposed with "pin-up" images of very young women. Few women are in editorial and byline positions.

- While strong, realistic images of women and of human sexuality are scarce, pornography and violent videos remain very popular and are widely available and used by young men. Canada has not yet found an effective means of stemming distribution of these harmful images.

- New technologies challenge the ability of any country to effectively regulate media. Materials often originate in foreign countries and cross borders via satellite or computer modem. Any serious attempt to eradicate violence from Canadian media will have to take these technologies into account and will require international co-operation.

- Women believe they have an essential role to play in preparing policy both for now and for the future and are currently denied this opportunity in a number ways.

New Orientations

All levels of government and all media organizations must co-operate to:

- adopt and implement zero tolerance;

- incorporate women's perspectives and experiences into all forms of media expression;

- publicly recognize the link between portrayal of violence against women and enactment of violence against women; and

- end sexual and racial stereotyping and expand the portrayal of women in their diversity.

Zero Tolerance Actions for All Organizations and Individuals in the Media Sector

Priority Setting and Allocation of Resources

M.1 Publicly recognize the significant role media play in either supporting or undermining women's equality and safety.

Human Resource Management

M.2 Ensure gender equity in hiring, in promotion, on editorial boards and in all aspects of media including technical areas and at all levels of management. Create timetables to reach gender equity in hiring within three years.

M.3 Evaluate working environments for women crew on location and provide safety supports where necessary.

M.4 Recruit women from different cultures and races and those with an understanding and sensitivity to the harms of sexism and racism and other acts and attitudes of discrimination.

M.5 Provide training on the latest research on violence and the value of its prevention as both a health promotion and crime prevention issue, and on the desensitizing impact of the media.

Legislation/Regulation/Policy

M.6 Rigorously apply sex-role stereotyping guidelines.

M.7 Create effective policies to eliminate gratuitous violence and sexist and racist portrayals that demean women, reduce sensationalism in the reporting of violence, and encourage accurate and sensitive reporting.

M.8 Develop policies that explicitly support women's and children's safety.

M.9 Realign policies throughout the organization to challenge the tolerance of violence and more explicitly support the equality of women and the prevention of violence.

Zero Tolerance Actions for Specific Organizations

All public and private broadcasters.

Programs/Services/Practices

M.10 Develop significantly more women's programming.

M.11 Create timetables to achieve gender balance in programming.

M.12 Ensure that cultural and historical representations include women in all their diversity including accurate historical representation of Aboriginal and Inuit women and their contributions to history.

M.13 Create programming on media literacy and on violence prevention.

M.14 Develop educational initiatives including distance learning packages on the less understood aspects of violence.

Consultation

M.15 Create women's programming with women's media organizations.

M.16 Include women at all stages of program development, delivery and evaluation. Conduct research with both current audiences and potential audiences.

M.17 Create program advisory boards with women experts.

M.18 Consult women's organizations on the positive uses of the new communication technologies.

Co-ordination

M.19 Develop, with women's organizations, pilot broadcasting projects that support women's safety.

M.20 Recognize the connection between depicted or described violence and its real counterpart.

M.21 Incorporate the work of anti-violence organizations into the work of the broadcaster.

M.22 Support Aboriginal and Inuit media and ethnic media in securing resources and through sharing of expertise and other resources.

Research and Evaluation

M.23 Expand data collection and analysis of programming using non-sexist, non-racist criteria of the Canadian Radio-television and Telecommunications Commission.

M.24 Regularly review research findings on violence for integration into policy development and programming.

M.25 Collect evaluations from diverse groups of women on the success of the media in reflecting their equality and safety concerns.

Educational/Promotional Activities

M.26 Initiate, with women's organizations and other community groups representing a range of cultures and races, co-operative educational activities for the public using the medium to support the message of the importance of preventing violence in terms of its human, social and financial costs.

Accountability

M.27 Create accessible processes to respond effectively to problems or complaints of sexism, racism and the treatment of issues of violence and women's safety.

M.28 Report at annual public meetings on the initiatives taken by the organization to support women's equality and the elimination of violence.

All print media organizations.

Human Resource Management

M.29 Develop proactive, culturally relevant initiatives such as hiring columnists to write on women's safety initiatives and aspects of zero tolerance.

Programs/Services/Practices

M.30 Dedicate print space as frequently as possible to the issues of violence, women's safety and equality.

Consultation

M.31 Consult with women's groups on expanding women's content in programming.

Research and Evaluation

M.32 Give resources and print space to data collection of women's perspectives on the impact of violence in their lives, the types and frequency of harassment and victimization they experience, the costs inherent in the tolerance of violence and the possible solutions. Include perspectives of women from a range of cultural backgrounds and races, all classes and ability levels.

All film and video organizations.

Human Resource Management

M.33 Promote gender equity through the allocation of resources for film and video development and production to women's production houses, women writers, producers and directors.

Legislation/Regulation/Policy

M.34 Eliminate sexist and racist practices in the development, production and distribution of films and videos including rock videos.

Programs/Services/Practices

M.35 Create opportunities in commercial enterprises to promote anti-violence initiatives and to include women at all stages of production.

M.36 Provide dedicated funding for women's production with fair portions dedicated to critically under-represented women, for example, Inuit and Aboriginal women.

Research and Evaluation

M.37 Allocate resources for data collection on less well understood aspects of women's safety and violence prevention, and equality.

M.38 Make public the figures on the support of women's production and the key messages delivered on violence and equality.

Educationa/Promotional Activities

M.39 Give priority to the use of film and video to expand understanding of the less well understood aspects of violence and the harm done by tolerating violence.

M.40 Use a portion of profits from commercial interests to develop media literacy programming.

All advertising agencies and advertisers.

Priority Setting/Allocation of Resources

M.41 Commit support to non-violent productions through advertising and sponsorship.

Programs/Services/Practices

M.42 Create anti-violence advertising for public service announcements and wherever possible in commercial work.

Research and Evaluation

M.43 Create focus groups and carry out market testing with women, taking care to represent the diversity of women in focus groups and other market research.

Education/Promotional Activities

M.44 Provide access to creative media production resources for development of public education anti-violence campaigns.

All voluntary organizations associated with media.

Legislation/Regulation/Policy

M.45 Create voluntary codes in press councils, broadcasters' associations, advertising foundations, women's media and other voluntary associations that explicitly recognize the importance of non-sexist, non-racist programming and practices as well as the value of violence prevention as a priority media activity.

Programs/Services/Practices

M.46 Develop in-service training for members and public education programming on the inter-relationship between media and violence.

M.47 Encourage members to donate air time or sponsor advertising for anti-violence against women campaigns through the Canadian Association of Broadcasters.

Consultation

M.48 Ensure participation of anti-violence organizations, women's equality seeking organizations, and member organizations in the creation of voluntary codes for broadcasting both on ending violence and on portrayal of women.

Co-ordination

M.49 Co-ordinate media partners and women's groups to create media campaigns against violence against women.

Research and Evaluation

M.50 Monitor the participation and portrayal of women in all their diversity in all aspects of media.

M.51 Fund women's organizations to do media analysis and research on women and the media.

Education/Promotional Activities

M.52 Create regular educational sessions for members and the public on the inter-relationships between women's equality, violence and the media; violence and women's health and the media's role in supporting community safety.

Accountability

M.53 Report publicly on initiatives undertaken to support equality and eliminate violence.

M.54 Create accessible complaints processes and ensure that those adjudicating complaints are appropriately trained.

All regulatory agencies and bodies.

Priority Setting/Allocation of Resources

M.55 Effectively regulate on ending violence in the media and on realistic portrayal of women in all their diversity in the media. Abandon self regulation if it cannot be made effective.

Legislation/Regulation/Policy

M.56 Build in, as a condition of licence for public broadcast, the obligation to provide programming to support women's equality, safety and the elimination of violence.

M.57 Pilot the provision of dedicated broadcast space for women through licensing.

M.58 Develop strong policy against depiction of gratuitous violence and degrading portrayals of women in all media and enforce it through licensing procedures.

Programs/Services/Practices

M.59 Create or support the creation of media literacy programming.

M.60 Recognize and give credit to non-violent programming at licence renewal.

M.61 Ensure the development of non-violent programming.

Consultation

M.62 Consult regularly with women's organizations on the impacts of media on women.

Co-ordination

M.63 Co-ordinate information from women and women's groups and studies on the links between women's safety and media violence. Share this information with regulated broadcasters.

Research and Evaluation

M.64 Monitor the portrayal of women through hearings, and other forms of data collection. Ensure monitoring takes into account sexism, racism, homophobia, age bias and prejudice against women with disabilities.

Education/Promotional Activities

M.65 Educate the public on complaints and regulatory processes to improve their access to these processes

Accountability

M.66 Report publicly on the initiatives undertaken to reduce sexism, racism and violence.

M.67 Report publicly on the use of regulation to support women's equality and safety.

M.68 Report publicly on the disposition of complaints related to women's equality and safety.

Federal, provincial and territorial governments.

Priority Setting/Allocation of Resources

M.69 Discuss issues of women and the media in international forums and work to establish international regulation of violence against women in the media.

M.70 Recognize the responsibility governments have to use their fiscal and other powers to support public safety interests, to promote equality of all women and the enjoyment of security by all women.

M.71 Fund Aboriginal and Inuit media to the level necessary to establish a strong media communication link within and among all peoples.

Human Resource Management

M.72 Appoint individuals to regulatory, governing and advisory boards who demonstrate clear understanding of equality issues and the interrelationships between inequality and violence and violence and the media.

Legislation/Regulation/Policy

M.73 Provide regulatory agencies to cover broadcast, film and video. Set clear standards that recognize the value of preventing violence, the significant role the media can play in supporting public safety and, in particular, women's safety interests and the promotion of equality.

M.74 Develop policies that reflect the link between violence in the media and violence in society that is supported by reviews of the literature and the research done by the Canadian Radio-television and Telecommunications Commission and the National Film Board.

Programs/Services/Practices

M.75 Expand support to those with a record of producing programming that incorporates equality issues such as the women's programs of the National Film Board.

M.76 Support the implementation of an industry-wide code on television violence that specifically addresses the unacceptability of depictions of violence against women. Extend the code where possible to video and other media.

M.77 Ensure that government advertising does not support sexist, racist or violent programming in any way.

Consultation

M.78 Initiate hearings on the impacts of media on women's equality and safety.

Details

- *Involve government, the industry and women's organization in the process.*

- *The terms of reference for the hearings should include the review and assessment of the effects of sexually violent media on women's and children's safety and security; the assessment and determination of the impact of new communication technologies on women's safety and equality and the impact of related media such as video games; and recommendations on how best to utilize and limit the use of the technologies; and the development of recommendations on the nature and depth of regulation needed for the various forms of media.*

Co-ordination

M.79 Create interdisciplinary advisory panels to monitor media and make the links between media, safety and equality issues.

M.80 Co-ordinate the input of provincial, territorial or local government hearings at the federal level to promote the co-operative development of national standards.

M.81 Work with other government initiatives aimed at ending violence against women.

Research and Evaluation

M.82 Collect data to improve recognition of the links between gender-equality issues, including sexism and sex-role stereotyping, women's safety and violence prevention, and, health promotion for women.

M.83 Collect and disseminate information on the new communication technologies.

M.84 Fund research to develop the most effective and culturally relevant public education programs on the prevention of violence against girls and women and the promotion of equality.

Education/Promotional Activities

M.85 Provide educational sessions on the data and research collected.

M.86 Support women's film and other media production of educational materials on women's safety and equality. Give priority to educational productions highlighting the safety issues for specific populations of women.

M.87 Support the development of media literacy materials for parents, specifically focusing on depictions of women on television and in films.

Accountability

M.88 Report at least annually on the initiatives related to media undertaken to promote equality and women's safety.

RELIGIOUS INSTITUTIONS

Introduction

In Canada, the predominant religious ideology has been Christian. The teachings of Christianity have greatly influenced our lives, directed our sexuality and left indelible marks on all aspects of our existence, even to the point of directing legal codes and many social conventions. Today, a diversity of other religions are also practised in Canada including Judaism, Islam, Hinduism, Buddhism and Sikhism. These faiths are an omnipresent and powerful force affecting all of us whether or not we follow the religious teachings.

Religious institutions have a long history of domination, control, and exploitation of women. Through theological teachings and by example, these institutions maintain and reinforce the belief that women are inferior to men and suited primarily to a domestic role. Many religions also attempt to control women's sexuality, reproductive rights and sexual orientation. In the name of religion, women have been diminished, enslaved, reduced to silence and relegated to the sidelines of progress and development.

Patriarchal instruction within religious institutions has encouraged and excused, both actively and passively, male violence against women in the home, in society and in the religious institutions them-selves. Strict rules of blind obedience to men and to religious teachings, posited as divine orders, have supported a dangerous power imbalance between women and men. Religious practices, rites, celebra-tions, language and symbolism all contribute to women's personal, political and social devaluation.

Very often women who have suffered male violence turn to religious advisors as their first and sometimes only confidante. They have been taught to acknowledge them as counsellors and spiritual guides who can ease pain, offer encouragement and intercede on their behalf with the Supreme Being. Women have trusted them. However, many women are now questioning the excessive influence of religious figures in matters of violence. They realize that predominantly male religious leaders do not understand the experience of violence against women nor its roots. Through lack of knowledge these leaders continue to provide women with dangerous direction that compromises their safety, leads to further revictimization and supports the tolerance of violence against them. This happens every time a woman is told to return to an abusive man.

Women have formed groups within religious structures to work toward the transformation of the institution into an egalitarian organization. Some women have become theologians, have studied the sacred books and have found alternative interpretations of words and laws that support equality of women. Increasingly, women are demanding an equal role with men, to be present on all decision-making bodies, to participate fully in the formulation of moral discourse and to be recognized as theologians in a true partnership. For some religions, women provide both the membership numbers and the support needed to sustain these institutions.

Women have a right to practice religion in an equal and safe atmosphere. Religious teachings and structures must be re-evaluated and altered to eliminate sexist and misogynist principles and practices.

Key Problems:

- In even the most progressive religions, structures remain bluntly anti-democratic. The hierarchical structure demands obedience of its members, facilitates the exercise of power and ensures the control of information. All-encompassing, unquestionable authority alienates women and makes equality a remote prospect.

- Some Christian churches still have much to answer for in their treatment of Aboriginal and Inuit peoples. The early missionaries, blind to the richness of the spiritual life of the Aboriginal and Inuit peoples, destroyed communities and brought physical, psychological, emotional and sexual violence to bear against many. Churches, along with the Canadian government, operated residential schools that separated Aboriginal and Inuit children from their parents and their communities and systematically forced these children to deny their spiritual, cultural and linguistic heritage.

- Some religious leaders have abused their positions of power and trust to sexually assault women and children. Such abuse results in profound trauma and lifelong guilt and confusion for the victim. Often abuse has been cloaked in secrecy making its continuation possible and conveying the false impression that the sexual exploitation of women and children does not exist in religious circles.

New Orientations for the Religious Sector

R.1 All religious institutions, at national, regional and community levels must acknowledge the fundamental equality of women and men, and work to revise religious teachings that promote inequality of women and support violence against women.

R.2 All religious institutions must adopt democratic structures to balance power between religious leaders and followers of the religion.

Zero Tolerance Actions for all Religious Institutions

Priority Setting/Allocation of Resources

R.3 Appoint an advisory committee of women from within the religious community to direct a comprehensive review of the teachings and structures that foster violence against women.

R.4 Direct resources to advisory committees to implement an action plan for achieving equality and ending violence.

Human Resource Management

R.5 Strengthen or adopt equity programs to achieve gender equality within all bodies. The diversity of people within the religious community served must be considered and represented.

R.6 Recruit staff who are knowledgeable about equality and about ending violence against women.

R.7 Provide training to all staff on women's inequality and its linkages to violence against women.

R.8 Remove from office or terminate the employment of any abusive spiritual leader, volunteer or staff member.

Programs/Services/Practices

R.9 Review all basic materials, training programs, videos and texts used for religious and relationship instruction to eliminate sexist, racist and homophobic images and messages.

R.10 Present discussion groups, workshops and seminars on violence against women. Include the linkages between inequality and violence.

R.11 Acknowledge and recognize the competence of feminist theologians and women members by incorporating the discourse of women into religious instruction.

R.12 In meetings with youth, emphasize equality of women and make it clear that the religious institution does not tolerate violence against women.

Co-ordination:

R.13 Appoint women's committees at all levels within the organization to co-ordinate actions on promoting equality and ending violence. Include feminist theologians, lay members of women's religious communities, volunteers from local communities and women working against violence.

R.14 Link prevention strategies with the wider secular community to remain current on resources and expertise.

Research and Evaluation

R.15 Together with the women's committees, evaluate each activity for progress toward achieving women's equality and ending violence.

R.16 Finance research activities by women who seek equality and are knowledgeable on violence against women to determine the prevalence and nature of this violence within the institution.

Accountability

R.17 Recognize that all abusers within the institution must withdraw from community service and no longer hold positions of trust and authority. Any board of inquiry on the conduct of a religious leader must include representatives of the women's committees. All decisions of such an inquiry must be made public.

R.18 Make all teaching materials used within the institution available to all community members.

R.19 Have the women's committees review all teachings to ensure the consistency of messages about women.

R.20 Recognize the injury to Aboriginal and Inuit people through the residential schools and make financial restitution to cover the costs of healing.

R.21 Recognize and respect the reclaiming of Aboriginal and Inuit spirituality by Aboriginal and Inuit peoples.

R.22   Acknowledge responsibility for any abuse done to victims within the institution and provide financial assistance for counselling programs and other forms of support for victims.

R.23   Make open decisions concerning the life of the religious community and include women and men equally in those decisions.

GOVERNMENT SECTOR

Introduction

The *Canadian Charter of Rights and Freedoms* guarantees equality to women, including the right to security of the person and equal benefit and protection of the law. All governments in Canada have the responsibility to assure these rights and the obligation to provide leadership to all others in Canada to uphold women's equality and safety. Throughout our consultations it was impressed upon us that governments in Canada, at all levels, are failing to live up to these responsibilities.

Key Problems:

- Government analysis does not recognize the full scope of woman abuse nor adequately link violence against women to women's unequal status in Canadian society. The absence of a strong equality framework has retarded progress towards full equality for women. Women have had too little participation in the workings of government, as elected officials, in senior policy positions and as key implementors.

- Policy consultation with women is relatively new – initiated only in the last two decades. It is often cursory in nature, is not representative of the diversity of women, and is carried out only when women's stake in the outcome is very apparent.

- There is still little understanding that all laws, policies and programs, regardless of the subject, have impacts on women as well as men.

- Government analysis is often gender neutral. Policies grounded in research that does not take into account the differential impacts of gender, race, class and abilities will persistently fail the needs of all women.

- Governments' actions on violence against women often cast anti-violence initiatives in terms of "family violence". As pointed out in Part I, defining violence against women in such terms, obscures the facts that the violence within families is overwhelmingly perpetrated by men against women, and it shares a common denominator of abuse of power with woman abuse in other settings. A "family violence" perspective ignores much violence against women outside the family, leads to gender-neutral analysis, and often places the focus on the family, rather than on the victim of violence.

- In rhetoric, governments have recognized that violence against women is a crime. However, policies and programs to deal with crime do not adequately reflect the criminal nature of woman abuse nor the size and nature of the problem. Often responses to sexual abuse including pornography are based on child protection, and ignore the harm done to women.

- Woman abuse crosses all jurisdictional boundaries, yet the division of powers within Canada makes effective response difficult. One of the largest sources of frustration reported during the Panel's consultations was the lack of clarity about jurisdictional responsibility and lack of co-ordination among jurisdictions in dealing with violence against women. Repeatedly we heard that jurisdictional disputes have blocked action that was urgently required.

- Government policies and practices are often sexist, racist and heterosexist and do not adequately take into account differences based on class, ability, age or geographic location.

- Aboriginal and Inuit peoples are particularly susceptible to deficiencies in government policy, especially at the federal level, since the lives of Aboriginal peoples are tightly regulated by government. Aboriginal and Inuit governments themselves have an impact on the lives of Aboriginal women. Policies that fail to take adequate account of culture and gender violate the rights of Aboriginal and Inuit women and have severely affected their safety and security.

- Violence against women is a violation of fundamental human rights. Globally, and in Canada, women's liberty is curtailed by violence; women's health and welfare are severely undermined by violence; and women die from violence. Canada prides itself on being a guardian and advocate of human rights at home and throughout the world. Despite public commitment, governments do not always take full account of violence against women when analysing human rights issues and designing human rights initiatives. The Government of Canada still does not adequately recognize woman abuse as a form of persecution and a genuine threat to women's life and liberty.

In other sector plans, specific actions are directed at various levels and specific departments of government, including Aboriginal and Inuit governments. The actions set out in this plan must be implemented in concert with all the others including the Equality Action Plan.

New Orientations for Governments — Federal, Provincial-Territorial, Municipal and Regional

G.1 Adopt and fully implement the Zero Tolerance Policy and the Equality Action Plan and establish the recommended accountability mechanisms.

Details:

- *Accountability mechanisms are outlined for the federal government in Section 4 of this plan. We recommend that the provincial and territorial governments adopt accountability mechanisms that parallel those proposed for the federal level. Municipalities should also develop accountability mechanisms that suit their structures and conform with the standards of accountability laid out in the Zero Tolerance Policy.*

- *Governments must require affected organizations (i.e., departments, agencies, boards, crown corporations, commissions) to develop and implement a plan for achieving the goals of zero tolerance and to report regularly to government and to women constituents on progress.*

- *Governments must provide information and support to the affected organizations for the development and implementation of the plan.*

G.2 Implement a zero tolerance contract compliance program whereby any organization which receives a government contract, grant or funding of $100,000 or more must agree to put in place zero tolerance processes and practices to support women's equality and safety within the recipient organization and through its substantive work.

Details:

• *The $100,000 criterion must be seen as a starting point with the long-term objective to have all organizations that have a fiscal relationship with government incorporate zero tolerance into their structures and work.*

• *Governments must set up the mechanisms and provide the resources to administer, provide support and monitor the compliance program.*

• *Governments must devise a means to monitor the compliance of affected organizations.*

New Orientations for Aboriginal and Inuit Governments

G.3 Adopt and fully implement the Zero Tolerance Policy and in partnership with Aboriginal and Inuit women's associations establish accountability mechanisms that will facilitate and monitor implementation of the Zero Tolerance Policy.

Zero Tolerance Actions Specifically for the Federal Government

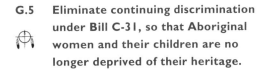

G.4 Provide financial and other resources to Aboriginal and Inuit women's organizations to ensure the full participation of Aboriginal and Inuit women at all stages of negotiation, development and implementation of self-government.

G.5 Eliminate continuing discrimination under Bill C-31, so that Aboriginal women and their children are no longer deprived of their heritage.

G.6 Create proactive programs to increase significantly the number of adult Aboriginal and Inuit women participating in post-secondary education and vocational training programs.

G.7 Enhance educational assistance provided by Indian and Northern Affairs Canada to extend additional support to Aboriginal women, especially for single mothers.

G.8 Make educational grants available to Métis and non-status women.

G.9 Fund an Aboriginal and Inuit women's office to receive and co-ordinate the distribution of government funds provided to Aboriginal communities to deal with violence against Aboriginal and Inuit women; to act as a clearing house for information on violence against women; and to provide assistance to women working in communities in developing programs and services.

G.10 Immediately implement all housing recommendations in the Fourth Report of the Standing Committee on Aboriginal Affairs

Details:

Include the following in Aboriginal housing policy:

- *Wherever consultation with Aboriginal organizations is specified in the development of new housing policies, the full and equal participation of equivalent Aboriginal women's organizations must be ensured, whether at the national, regional or local level.*

- *All home ownership programs must ensure the full protection of women's property rights.*

- *Any and all bodies and organizations involved in the delivery of Aboriginal housing must ensure equal representation of Aboriginal women.*

- *Transfer of resources by government to any administrative body(ies) must ensure the full participation of women at all stages, with accountability to Aboriginal women's organizations.*

- *Data collection, program delivery, policy and program decisions must engage the full and equal participation of Aboriginal women.*

- *In conjunction with Ministerial Guarantees for housing, financial institutions must ensure equality of applications made by women, and women's property rights must be entrenched in all transactions.*

- *Housing needs must be determined by the community, with the full and equal participation of women from that community.*

G.11 Have women who are immigrating to Canada deal directly with immigration officers rather than communicating through their male relatives.

Details:

- *Apprise these women of their rights in Canada.*

- *Ensure that there are women immigration officials to deal with women where this is culturally dictated.*

G.12 Provide information regarding violence against women in Canada and programs, services and protections that a woman may use directly to women in their own language upon arrival in Canada.

G.13 Ensure that every woman who is new to Canada has a contact she can call upon if faced with violence.

G.14 Abolish the current Live-in Caregiver Program and replace it with changes in the immigration assessment system which place a higher value on care-giving occupations and associated qualifications.

G.15 Recognize violence against women as a human rights issue.

G.16 Include violence against women as an issue in all human rights decisions and initiatives, both nationally and internationally.

G.17 Include violence against women as an issue in all international aid and development activities.

G.18 Create guidelines for the establishment of any future inquiries, task forces, or commissions.

Details:

- The proposed mandate, rules and operating procedures of any commission of inquiry or panel similar to the Canadian Panel on Violence Against Women must be outlined as clearly as possible before such a body is established.

- Mechanisms must be introduced to enable future members of such bodies to contact each other and exchange views on the nature of their duties and mandate before they are officially appointed.

- Mechanisms must be established to enable such members to assume responsibility for the refinement of their mandate and they must be given the time and opportunity to examine and negotiate its terms and conditions before they take up their duties.

- New mechanisms for consultations between the federal government and women's groups in Canada, based on a vision of social change, must be established as soon as possible.

- Mechanisms must be developed which would guarantee better representation of all population groups in Canada in projects similar to this Panel.

Zero Tolerance Actions Specifically for Municipal and Regional Governments

G.19 Implement an urban safety program that makes women's safety a priority at the municipal level.

Details:

- Design all public and semi-public spaces such as parks, streets and municipal properties to reduce opportunity for assaults on women.

- Use municipal by-laws to regulate display of sexually violent material.

- Develop community safety initiatives such as Safe City Committees which place a high priority on ending violence against women.

Zero Tolerance Actions for Aboriginal and Inuit Governments

G.20 Develop an Aboriginal Charter of Rights with the full participation of Aboriginal and Inuit women's associations. Until such time as the Charter Is developed and Implemented, *the Canadian Charter of Rights and Freedoms* is to apply as a minimum protection for Aboriginal and Inuit women and children.

G.21 Reform the political structures of all Aboriginal organizations at all levels so they are truly representative and fully accountable to Aboriginal women.

G.22 Establish a gender-equity employment program to equalize participation of Aboriginal and Inuit women.

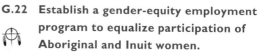

SECTION 4

MONITORING AND ACCOUNTABILITY MECHANISMS

The Panel places a very high priority on measures which ensure that actions are undertaken to end violence against women and to assure their safety. Accountability – through open processes and in accordance with zero tolerance standards – is essential.

It is imperative that this National Action Plan be considered carefully, amended and expanded where appropriate, implemented, then monitored and evaluated on a regular basis.

The National Action Plan indicates that many participants must take a role in ending violence against women and promoting their equality. However, the federal government, as initiator of the Panel, has a special responsibility to respond quickly and comprehensively, by adopting the Zero Tolerance Policy, by making specific commitments to implement the National Action Plan and by helping to mobilize the support of the other partners indicated in the Plan.

To ensure that the National Action Plan receives support and that progress is both made and measured, the Panel proposes the following accountability framework.

1. Principles

• Incorporate the knowledge, experience and perspectives of individuals and groups in the non-governmental sector, i.e., service providers, front-line workers and women's organizations who have provided leadership in the provision of services for victims of violence and in violence prevention work.

• Establish a comprehensive monitoring capacity to assess, both collectively and individually, the impact of the many different departments with programs, policies and legislation pertaining to the issue of violence against women.

• Provide mechanisms at several levels to assess activities. No single mechanism can adequately monitor all activities to end violence against women in Canada.

• Strengthen the monitoring and accountability functions of existing mechanisms. Create new ones as required.

• Ensure that the composition and scope of work of these mechanisms are represenative and inclusive.

2. Objectives

• Ensure that the federal government considers the National Action Plan and responds with a clear statement of commitment in a timely fashion – no later than three months after the tabling of the Panel's final report.

- Ensure that initiatives of the federal government which have the potential to address violence against women – for example, the Canadian Strategy on Community Safety and Crime Prevention – place a high priority on violence against women and adopt a zero tolerance approach to their work and their recommendations.

- Ensure that government departments adopt a zero tolerance approach in their internal processes and their substantive work.

3. Functions

- Monitor and assess the implementation of the measures set out in the National Action Plan on a regular basis.

- Assess the scope, extent and nature of violence against women, including periodic surveys to establish whether violence is increasing or decreasing, which types of violence are increasing or decreasing and changes in the vulnerability of particular groups or populations.

- Assess the effectiveness and impact of measures taken to end violence against women by the federal government, other levels of government and non-governmental organizations.

- Assess progress on gender equality in Canada, particularly those aspects of equality which would reduce vulnerability to violence.

- Recommend additions to the National Action Plan, including pilot testing of innovative solutions.

- Report publicly on all of the above to ensure follow-up by the appropriate agencies and authorities.

4. Mechanisms

The Equality Plan includes several proposals which are vital to a comprehensive accountability framework, namely, the enactment of a status of women act to strengthen the government's commitment to gender equality and issues related to violence against women; the designation of a senior minister responsible for the status of women who would also be the lead minister for violence against women issues; a strengthened department at the federal level responsible for the status of women; the creation of a permanent advisory board to advise the government on its equality and safety plans; and the provision of sufficient resources to non-governmental women's organizations to permit their effective participation in policy development.

In addition, the Panel considers the following accountability mechanisms to be essential to ensure implementation and evaluation of the National Action Plan and the Canadian campaign to end violence against women.

- **Elevation of the Sub-committee on the Status of Women to full parliamentary committee status, with responsibility for regular review of progress toward implementation of the National Action Plan and the federal government's commitment to ending violence against women.**

  Parliamentary committees can be provided with authority, responsibility and resources to undertake comprehensive reviews of government programs and legislation. (For example, the Employment Equity Act requires that reviews be conducted within five years of enactment and every three years thereafter). In response to an open call for submissions, any individual or group can provide testimony to a parliamentary committee. As the committee reports directly to Parliament, the opportunity exists for extensive political and public debate on the adequacy of measures already taken, and on proposals for new programs, policies and legislation.

When the committee undertakes this review, it should be reconstituted as a special committee with an expanded mandate and the resources necessary to fulfil that mandate, including the means to hold meetings outside Ottawa and to have experts and representatives of organizations in the non-governmental sector participate.

• **Creation by the federal government of a zero tolerance accountability board with a mandate to review and assess progress at the federal level on implementation of the National Action Plan. As the primary on-going accountability mechanism, the board would ensure that the federal government receives independent advice on a regular basis on the effectiveness of its actions to end violence against women. It would comprise members from federal government departments with responsibility for the issue of violence against women, and individuals from the non-governmental sector – with the latter being the majority. Two co-chairs would represent the government and non-governmental sectors. Secretariat services would be provided by the department within the federal government with lead and co-ordinating responsibility for violence against women issues.**

The board would meet at least three times a year, set its own agenda and process for review of progress by the federal government and would issue a report biennially to be tabled in Parliament. On request from the federal government, the board could review particular issues and provide advice to the minister and the government. It would rely on the knowledge

and experience of its members, information gathered by the departmental secretariat from federal departments and/or other sources inside and outside the government – in particular the Centres of Excellence and other non-governmental organizations involved in service provision, violence prevention or research.

While the board would focus primarily on actions taken by the federal government, it would be encouraged to assess federal government action in the larger social context as well.

The board would have a fixed term of eight years to ensure implementation of the National Action Plan and the meeting of the Plan's objectives by the year 2000.

• **Creation by provincial and territorial governments of zero tolerance accountability boards modelled on the federal approach. Provincial and territorial governments have significant responsibilities in the campaign to end violence against women. Monitoring and evaluation are required to assess action taken at this level.**

Zero tolerance accountability boards at the provincial/territorial level would operate in much the same way as has been proposed for the federal level. Membership from both governmental and non-governmental sectors and public reporting on a regular basis are essential.

A CALL TO ACTION FOR ALL MEN AND WOMEN

Introduction

Violence against women is pervasive in Canada. We each have a story to tell: a girl molested by her uncle, a best friend whose ex-boyfriend is stalking her, an older woman who can't explain the bruises. These incidents affect us profoundly. They make us fearful for our children, wary about our own activities and often distrustful of men.

The connection between these acts of violence and the inequality of women is clear. All women in Canada are vulnerable to male violence. Race, class, age, sexual orientation, level of ability and other objective characteristics, alone or in combination, compound the risk. Until all women achieve equality they will remain vulnerable to violence, and until women are free from violence, they cannot be equal.

We have called on governments and institutions to change how they operate, to seek equality for women and to end violence against women. We now appeal to you, as an individual, to help change the status quo.

What Can I Do?

As friends, parents, children, neighbours, students, colleagues and community members we have responsibilities and opportunities to make change. The following section suggests ways you can support our National Action Plan and our goals — to achieve equality for women and to put an end to violence against women.

Many of you are already working as volunteers or staff members in women's shelters, rape crisis centres or in other services for victims and survivors. To you, we give our respect and support. Others are very committed and concerned but live busy lives leaving little time for activism and volunteer work. We offer some suggestions on how you can contribute.

We also know that some of you are active in working for equality for women and in men's groups to eliminate violence in society. You are part of the solution.

However, some men feel that the issues of equality and ending violence are not relevant to them. They may have many excuses.

- I am only concerned about violence in general; I do not feel it is right to focus on violence specifically against women.

- Violence against women is a women's issue.

- Women have achieved true equality and I don't believe this is a problem.

- I am tired of hearing about violence against women, and I think the statistics and stories are exaggerated.

- Feminists are out to destroy all men; most women don't even like feminists.

- I don't beat my wife and I don't sexually abuse my daughter so this issue is not my problem.

- I am concerned about some of these problems but there is nothing I can do.

- I am a victim too. I witnessed plenty of violence in my own life, and there's little I can do about it now.

If you agreed with any of these statements, you are not alone. You represent millions of Canadian men who do not really understand the issues involved. You may have listened to women share feelings and experiences but did not relate to the problem. Most men react with denial and defensiveness about this topic. The reality is so painful that it is easier to believe that the problem does not exist or that each case represents some isolated incident. Rationalizations are invented which allow those with power to keep things the way they are.

We need all men in Canada to make a clear commitment to women's equality and to ending all forms of violence against women. We deserve a Canadian society that will no longer tolerate the daily acts of violence against women. Is this an impossible dream or can it be a future Canadian reality? Can all men accept the challenge to examine their behaviour as individuals and as members of a community? We believe they can. Many are doing so already.

Personal Action Plan

Women or men, of any age:

You can make a positive contribution to women's equality and ending violence against women by examining your own values, the life choices you make and your behaviour, as an individual or as a member of a particular group within your workplace, your community or Canadian society at large.

We call upon you to make a personal commitment to the principles of zero tolerance — that no amount of violence is acceptable and that women's safety is a priority — and we urge you to take action now. A little action from each of us will make such a difference.

In the following paragraphs, we identify how you can turn your commitment into action.

I will:

- Acknowledge that violence is a reality for at least half the women in Canada; recognize the tolerance of violence that keeps so much of it in place.

- Create my own action plan. Decide how I can help all the organizations I am connected with become zero tolerance organizations. Choose which actions I will actively support and decide how.

Some Ways I Can Get Started

As a man, I will:

- Not be violent.

- Give up my need for power and control.

- Promote equality, not only in thought and words, but in deeds.

- Listen to the women in my life — my mother, daughters, partners, friends, neighbours and colleagues.

- Ask women about their experiences, their fears and the equality barriers they face.

- Attend community forums on violence against women and listen to the women.

- Listen. Listen some more.

- Never argue with, minimize or deny women's feelings.

- Commit to act on what I learn.

- Talk to other men to seek support.

- Never listen to men who ridicule me or make me feel like "less of a man" for working to end violence against women.

- Share responsibility for child care and home maintenance and do my part without being asked.

- Challenge any tolerance of violence or sexist behaviour.

- Give financial and political support to services for victims and survivors of violence.

- Help victims and survivors return to the state they enjoyed before the crime.

- Teach my children that violence is an abuse of power and trust and does not resolve conflicts in relationships.

- Speak out on dating violence and inequality of women.

- Never purchase nor use pornography.

- Volunteer to work in a men's support group.

- Support women who are working to end violence.

- Challenge the backlash against women who are working toward equality and toward the ending of violence.

- Ensure that no woman and no child live in silence with violence in my home or in my neighbourhood.

- Challenge other men to become part of the solution.

As a woman or man who wants to end violence against women, I will:

- Remove power and control from my list of needs.

- Practice co-operation instead of competition.

- Not laugh at women-hating jokes and racial slurs.

- Stop believing stereotypes.

- Become more knowledgeable about racism and act on that knowledge.

- Support a fully accessible culture for all women.

- Learn the true history of Aboriginal and Inuit peoples.

- Inform myself on the current realities of life for Aboriginal and Inuit peoples.

- Resist and work to eliminate heterosexism.

- Refuse to respond to aggression with aggression.

- Support equal pay for work of equal value.

- Insist that Canada builds an accessible, affordable child-care program.

- Hire a woman for the job.

- Become media literate so I can decode harmful messages about women and about violence.

- Stop denying that violence against women exists or that it's only "those women."

- Never blame women for the violence in their lives.

- Understand that the only reason I am not in an abusive relationship is by luck — not because of my race, class or ability.

- Pay attention to a child who is hurting.

- Realize that children who witness violence suffer as much as those who are actually hit.

- Believe that I don't have to go through it alone.

- Hold violent people accountable for their choice to perpetuate violence.

- Speak up!

- Take time to know what I am feeling.

- Make peace with my past.

- Talk with a woman about the reality of her life.

- Share my story.

- Believe in myself.

- Thank a woman who helped me grow.

- Resist male-defined standards of beauty.

Consumer Action

As a consumer, I will:

- Challenge the tolerance of violence and sexism in movies, rock videos, magazines, on television and radio, and all advertising.

- Boycott movies and other media that glorify violence.

- Purchase non-violent, non-sexist toys.

- Stop buying products from advertisers who exploit women in their promotions.

- Read books by women of all races.

Family Action

In my family life, I will:

- Listen to my children and try to understand their perspectives.

- Commit to non-violent problem solving and discipline and learn how to follow through on that commitment.

- Find out what my children and grandchildren are watching on television.

- Share with my partner in the management and control of all family finances.

- Encourage my daughters and granddaughters to pursue all interests, including those which are non-traditional.

Neighbourhood Action

As a neighbour, I will:

- Stop denying that violence exists in my neighbourhood.

- Reach out to a neighbour who is isolated.

Workplace Action

In my workplace, I will:

- Find out what my employer is doing concerning equality and violence against women.

- Refrain from abusing my co-workers.

- Take time to know if an employee is being abused and offer support.

- Promote awareness and awareness sessions on violence against women.

Student Action

In my school, I will:

- Urge teachers and administrators to support gender-aware violence prevention activities.

- Treat my co-students with respect.

- Promote and practice equality.

- Get involved in working out alternatives to violence.

- Not put girls down.

- Support someone who is being hurt.

Community Action

In my community, I will:

- Help my community recognize that ending violence against women is a priority.

- Find out what services exist for victims of violence.

- Work with others to fill gaps in service.

- Actively discourage violence in sports.

- Ask my family doctor to display posters and pamphlets on violence against women.

- Insist that the school make gender-aware violence prevention part of its core curriculum.

- Spend time with children who could use support and a little fun.

- Contact my local transition house, rape crisis centre, other women's groups and ask how I can learn and help.

- Get a local men's service club to sponsor a community awareness session for men on violence issues.

- Challenge local service groups to become partners in ending violence.

- Write a letter to the editor of my community newspaper in support of ending violence.

- Challenge my municipal, provincial and federal politicians to practice zero tolerance.

- Talk about equality and violence against women in my place of worship.

- Start safety audits.

For those of you who wish to take a more public and active role in ending violence against women in your community, we have developed the Community Kit. It will help you to determine the nature and extent of violence in your community and to improve the services available to women victims/survivors. It will also help you to make your community safer for women and for all those who feel vulnerable to violence.

We had the unique opportunity and privilege to meet women from coast to coast to coast in Canada who had experienced violence in their lives. What impressed us most was their courage and their strength in coming forward. They shared the most intimate and difficult details of their lives and the violence they have endured, and they urged action. We share both their pain and their hopes and we encourage you to do your part to make Canada safe and equal for all women.

APPENDICES

A P P E N D I X   A

CONSULTATION EVENTS

A. PHASE I

The Panel used an interactive and community-based approach to conduct its first round of consultations. There were seven tours: British Columbia/Alberta; Québec; Atlantic; Ontario; Saskatchewan/Manitoba; NWT/Yukon; and, Northern Quebec/Labrador. The Panel set out to visit 100 communities and ultimately held consultations in 139. The Panel met approximately 4000 individuals.

BRITISH COLUMBIA/ALBERTA

January 17, 1992

VANCOUVER, British Columbia
- Shaughnessy Hospital
- Belbrook Community Centre

RICHMOND, British Columbia
- Atira Transition House

BURNABY, British Columbia
- British Columbia Institute of Family Violence

January 18, 1992

VANCOUVER, British Columbia
- Vancouver Aboriginal Friendship Centre
- Justice Institute of British Columbia

BURNABY, British Columbia
- Multicultural Services for Battered Women

CHILLIWACK, British Columbia
- Chilliwack Community Services Centre,
- St. Thomas Anglican Church
- Upper Fraser Valley Transition Society

VICTORIA, British Columbia
- Victoria RCMP Subdivision

January 19, 1992

VANCOUVER, British Columbia
- WAVAW (Woman Against Violence Against Women)

January 20

ALKALI LAKE, British Columbia
- Alkali Lake Reserve

WILLIAMS LAKE, British Columbia
- Women's Shelter

QUESNEL, British Columbia
- Amata Transition House

VANCOUVER, British Columbia
- Crab Tree Corner Support Centre for Single Mums
- YWCA
- Office of Battered Women's Support Services
- Amata House

BURNABY, British Columbia
- Burnaby Correctional Centre for Women

COURTENAY, British Columbia
- Kinhut
- Dountenay Transition Society

KAMLOOPS, British Columbia
- Kamloops Sexual Assault Counselling Centre,
- McArthur Park Community Centre
- Kamloops Immigrant Services Society
- RCMP Detachment Offices
- University College of the Cariboo
- Coast Canadian Inn

January 21

SMITHERS, British Columbia
- Passage Transition House
- Native Friendship Centre

PRINCE GEORGE, British Columbia
- Phoenix Transition House

RICHMOND, British Columbia
- Richmond Women's Resource Centre (Gateway Theatre)

VANCOUVER, British Columbia
- Society of Transition Houses for British Columbia and the Yukon

ROUND LAKE, British Columbia
- Round Lake Native Treatment Centre

VERNON, British Columbia
- Communities Against Sexual Assault

KELOWNA, British Columbia
- Central Okanogan Elizabeth Fry Society
- Kelowna Family Centre
- Kelowna Women's Shelter

January 22

HIGH PRAIRIE, Alberta
- High Prairie Native Friendship Centre

HINTON, Alberta
- Recreation Centre

CALGARY, Alberta
- International Hotel of Calgary

ST. MARY'S, British Columbia
- St. Mary's Indian Reserve, Band Office

CRANBROOK, British Columbia
- Cranbrook Community Action Centre

January 23

GRANDE PRAIRIE, Alberta
- Northern Addiction Centre

HINTON, Alberta
- Recreation Centre

RED DEER, Alberta
- Central Alberta Women's Emergency Shelter
- City R.C.M.P. Detachment
- Rocky Mountain House Community Centre
- Women's Outreach Centre

MEDICINE HAT, Alberta
- Medicine Hat Provincial Building
- Medicine Hat Women's Shelter Society

TABER, B.C.
- Family and Community Social Services Building

January 24, 1992

FORT McMURRAY, Alberta
- Provincial Building

CAMROSE, Alberta
- St. Mary's Hospital

ST. PAUL, Alberta
- County Office

GLEICHEN, Alberta
- Gleichen Reserve

MORLEY, Alberta
- Eagle's Nest Shelter on the Morley Reserve

CALGARY, Alberta
- International Hotel of Calgary
- Old Y Centre
- Calgary Women's Emergency Shelter Association
- Discovery House

PINCHER CREEK, Alberta
- Labelle Mansion

BROCKETT, Alberta
- Band Council Office, Brockett-Peigan Reserve

LETHBRIDGE, Alberta
- Sundance Inn
- YWCA

January 25

SHERWOOD PARK, Alberta
• A. J. Ottewell Centre (The Barn)

EDMONTON, Alberta
• Edmonton Public Library
• Women's Emergency Accommodation
  Centre

CALGARY, Alberta
• Women's Emergency Accommodation
  Centre
• Old Y Centre

BLOOD, Alberta
• Standoff-Blood Reserve, Shot Boat Side
  Building

Q U E B E C

February 9, 1992

QUEBEC CITY
• Centre communautaire services diocésains

February 10, 1992

QUEBEC CITY
• Centre Femmes d'aujourd'hui
• C.L.S.C. Basseville
• La table du roi
• Centre communautaire services diocésains

LA TUQUE
• C.L.S.C. Haut St. Maurice

STE-FOY
• Université Laval, Pavillon Jean Durand
  (C.E.Q.)

STE-FLAVIE (MONT JOLI), QUEBEC
• Motel La Gaspésiana

BAIE COMEAU
• C.L.S.C. D'Aquillon

February 11, 1992

SEPT-ILES
• C.L.S.C. de Sept-Iles

MISTASSINI
• Band Council Office, Mistassini Lake

CHISASIBI
• Women's Shelter

LEBEL-SUR-QUÉVILLON
• Lebel Health Centre/Centre de Santé Lebel

VAL D'OR
• Le Mi-Nordet C.L.S.C.

February 12, 1992

JONQUIÈRE
• Hôtel Roussillon

ROBERVAL
• Château Roberval

POVUNGNITUK
• Povungnituk Hospital

VILLE-MARIE
• Ville-Marie Women's Centre

February 13, 1992

ROUYN-NORANDA
• Hôtel-Motel Rouyn-Noranda

MONTREAL
• Centre St-Pierre
• YWCA
• Les ateliers d'éducation populaire de
  Mercier
• Centre Préfontaine
• Passages
• Simone de Beauvoir Institute
• Centre interculturel Strathearn

LAVAL
• CHOC Laval

February 14, 1992

MONTREAL
- Hôtel Delta
- Tribunal de la jeunesse
- Centre St-Pierre
- Maison Tanguay, Correctional Centre for Women
- Elizabeth Fry Society
- Catholic Community Services
- YWCA West-Island (Pointe-Claire)

SHERBROOKE
- L'Escale de L'Estrie (Sherbrooke)

February 15, 1992

HULL
- C.L.S.C de Hull

ATLANTIC REGION

March 1, 1992

ST. JOHN'S, Newfoundland
- Radisson Hotel

March 2, 1992

ST. JOHN'S, Newfoundland
- Patrick House
- Department of Mines and Energy, Confederation Building
- Hotel Newfoundland
- Iris Kirby House

STEPHENVILLE, Newfoundland
- St. Georges Women's Centre

GANDER, Newfoundland
- Sinbad's Hotel

NAIN, Labrador
- Labrador Inuit Association
- Town Hall

SAINT JOHN, New Brunswick
- Saint John Hilton
- Hestia House

March 3, 1992

NAIN, Labrador
- Grenfell Nursing Station
- Nain Group Home

GOOSE BAY, Labrador
- Aurora Hotel
- Libra House

BATHURST, New Brunswick
- Atlantique Host

BIG COVE, New Brunswick
- Big Cove Reserve, Child and Family Services

BURNT CHURCH, New Brunswick
- Burnt Church Reserve, Burnt Church Band Council Office

NEWCASTLE, New Brunswick
- Town Hall

FREDERICTON, New Brunswick
- University of New Brunswick Campus, Ludlow Hall

March 4, 1992

MONCTON, New Brunswick
- Conseil consultatif sur la condition de la femme du Nouveau-Brunswick
- Hôtel Beauséjour Restaurant

HALIFAX, Nova Scotia
- Bryony House

FREDERICTON, New Brunswick
- University of New Brunswick Campus
- Sheraton Hotel

March 5, 1992

TRURO, Nova Scotia
- Cox Institute, Nova Scotia Agricultural College

SUMMERSIDE, Prince Edward Island
- East Prince Women's Information Centre

O'LEARY, Prince Edward Island
- Regional Services Centre, Evangeline School

NEW GLASGOW, Nova Scotia
- Trinity United Church

ANTIGONISH, Nova Scotia
- Saint Francis Xavier University

CHARLOTTETOWN, Prince Edward Island
- Rape Crisis Centre
- Charlottetown Hotel
- Richmond Hotel
- McMillan Building
- Anderson House

March 6, 1992

KENTVILLE, Nova Scotia
- Kentville Recreation Centre

BRIDGEWATER, Nova Scotia
- South Shore Regional Hospital
- Capt. Wm. Spry Community Centre

HALIFAX, Nova Scotia
- Service for Sexual Assault Victims
- Adsum House
- Veith House
- North End Library

SYDNEY, Nova Scotia
- Every Woman's Women's Centre

ONTARIO

March 22, 1992

TORONTO, Ontario
- St. Lawrence Town Hall

March 23, 1992

TORONTO, Ontario
- St. Lawrence Town Hall

WINDSOR, Ontario
- Windsor Public Library
- Sexual Assault Crisis Centre

CHATHAM, Ontario
- Family Services Kent

TIMMINS, Ontario
- Venture Inn
- Hotel Senator

NORTH BAY, Ontario
- Empire Hotel Boardroom

March 24, 1992

TORONTO, Ontario
- St. Lawrence Town Hall

GODERICH, Ontario
- Survival Through Friendship House (shelter)
- Phoenix of Huron
- Huron County Museum
- Saugeen First Nations Reserve

NORTH BAY, Ontario
- Empire Hotel

SUDBURY, Ontario
- Northbury Hotel

March 25, 1992

BARRIE, Ontario
- Barrie City Hall

GUELPH, Ontario
- Steelworkers Hall

LONDON, Ontario
- Sexual Assault Centre, Shelby Building

OWEN SOUND, Ontario
- Second Stage Housing
- Children's Aid Society

COLLINGWOOD, Ontario
- Town Hall

ORANGEVILLE, Ontario
- Orangeville and District Senior Centre

THUNDER BAY, Ontario
- Airlane Hotel

SIOUX LOOKOUT, Ontario
- Nishnawbe-Gamik Friendship Centre

March 26, 1992

LONDON, Ontario
- Intercommunity Health Centre
- Glen Cairn Public School
- Somerville House, University of Western Ontario
- Atenlos Family Violence Centre
- Battered Women's Advocacy Centre

PETERBOROUGH, Ontario
- Women's Health Care Centre

CAMPBELLFORD, Ontario
- Warkworth Penitentiary

KINGSTON, Ontario
- Community House For Self-Reliance

OTTAWA, Ontario
- Holiday Inn
- St. John The Evangelist Anglican Church
- Public Service Alliance Building

BIG TROUT LAKE, Ontario
- Infirmerie

March 27, 1992

KINGSTON, Ontario
- Prison for Women (P4W)
- Kings Community House for Self-Reliance

WOODSTOCK, Ontario
- Ingamo Family Homes

HAMILTON, Ontario
- YWCA

OTTAWA, Ontario
- Holiday Inn
- St. John The Evangelist Anglican Church

THUNDER BAY, Ontario
- Airlane Hotel

S A S K A T C H E W A N / M A N I T O B A

April 7, 1992

SASKATOON, Saskatchewan
- Family Support Centre
- Saskatoon Centennial Auditorium

April 8, 1992

THE PAS, Manitoba
- Town Hall

WINNIPEG, Manitoba
- Manitoba Advisory Council on the Status of Women
- Women's Employment Counselling Service
- Women's Health Clinic
- Pluri-elles
- Manitoba Federation of Labour, Union Centre
- Family Law Section of the Manitoba Bar

PRINCE ALBERT, Saskatchewan
- Marlboro Inn

SASKATOON, Saskatchewan
- National Native Alcohol & Drug Abuse Program
- Saskatoon Indian & Metis Friendship Centre
- Family Support Centre
- Saskatoon Interval House
- Centennial Auditorium

April 9, 1992

THOMPSON, Manitoba
- YM/YWCA
- Mystery Lake Hotel

DAUPHIN, Manitoba
- Dr. Vern L. Watson Art Centre
- Parkland Crisis Centre

BRANDON, Manitoba
- Royal Oak Inn, Kensington Room

LA RONGE, Saskatchewan
- La Ronge Motor Inn/Hotel

SASKATOON, Saskatchewan
- Centennial Auditorium
- Immigrant Women of Saskatchewan and Immigrant Women of Saskatoon
- Saskatoon Mental Health Clinic

April 10, 1992

CROSS LAKE, Manitoba
- Town Hall

BRANDON, Manitoba
- Royal Oak Inn, Kensington Room
- YWCA Westman Women's Shelter

MORDEN, Manitoba
- Royal Canadian Legion Hall

MELFORD, Saskatchewan
- Heritage Inn
- The North East Crisis Intervention Centre

SANDY LAKE, Saskatchewan
- Sandy Lake Indian Reserve, Sandy Lake Hall

NORTH BATTLEFORD, Saskatchewan
- North Battleford Friendship Centre
- Battleford Indian Health Centre
- Battleford and Area Sexual Assault Centre
- Battleford Interval House

April 11, 1992

CHURCHILL, Manitoba
- Community Centre

SELKIRK, Manitoba
- Women's Centre
- Friendship Centre

FORT ALEXANDER, Manitoba
- Fort Alexander Reserve, Multipurpose Building

LAC DU BONNET, Saskatchewan
- Library Community Hall

MEADOW LAKE, Saskatchewan
- Northwestern Motel

MOOSE JAW, Saskatchewan
- Moose Jaw Transition House

SWIFT CURRENT, Saskatchewan
- Southwest Safe Shelter

April 12, 1992

PORTAGE LA PRAIRIE, Manitoba
- Herman Prior Seniors' Centre

LUNDAR, Manitoba
- Lutheran Church Hall

PRINCE ALBERT, Saskatchewan
- Pinegrove Correctional Center

YORKTON, Saskatchewan
- Yorkton Friendship Centre
- Holiday Inn
- Yorkton Mental Health Centre, Yorkton Union Hospital

April 13, 1992

WINNIPEG, Manitoba
- Manitoba Advisory Council on the Status of Women
- A private home
- Osborne House
- Women's Post Treatment Centre
- Children's Home of Winnipeg
- POWER (Prostitutes and other Women for Equal Rights)
- Holiday Inn Crowne Plaza

REGINA Saskatchewan
- Circle Project
- Regina Transition Women's Society
- Senior's Education Center, University of Regina: Old College Campus
- Social Services, Family Services Bureau

FORT QU'APPELLE, Saskatchewan
- Squire Hotel

April 14, 1992

WINNIPEG, Manitoba
- Holiday Inn Crowne Plaza Winnipeg

Northwest Territories/ Yukon

April 28, 1992

YELLOWKNIFE, Northwest Territories
- Northern United Place

April 29, 1992

YELLOWKNIFE, Northwest Territories
- Northern United Place
- Yellowknife Inn
- Tree of Peace Friendship Centre
- N'Dilo Community Hall

INUVIK, Northwest Territories
- Family Hall

FORT RAE, Northwest Territories
- Fort Rae-Edzo Friendship Centre
- Edzo Community Hall

WHITEHORSE, Yukon
- Whitehorse Correctional Centre
- Victoria Faulkner Women's Centre
- Yukon Inn
- Law Court Building

April 30, 1992

RANKIN INLET, Northwest Territories
- Siniktarvik Hotel

YELLOWKNIFE, Northwest Territories
- Explorer Hotel

INUVIK, Northwest Territories
- Family Hall
- Elementary and High School

FORT SMITH, Northwest Territories
- Pelican Rapids Inn
- Town Council Chambers
- McDougall Community Centre

TESLIN, Yukon
- Old Community Centre Building

WATSON LAKE, Yukon
- Help & Hope Shelter

DAWSON CITY, Yukon
- Dawson City Museum
- Band Office

May 1, 1992

IQALUIT, Northwest Territories
- Frobisher Inn
- Visitors Centre, New Library Building

FORT SMITH, Northwest Territories
- Pelican Rapids Inn

HAY RIVER, Northwest Territories
- Diamond Jenness High School
- Adult Education Centre
- Soaring Eagle Friendship Centre

WATSON LAKE, Yukon
- Help & Hope Shelter

OLD CROW, Yukon
- Yukon College

DAWSON CITY, Yukon
- Dawson City Museum

May 2,1992

IQALUIT, Northwest Territories
- Nutaraq Place (Shelter)
- Frobisher Inn, Husky Lounge
- Anglican Parish Hall

CAMBRIDGE BAY, Northwest Territories
- Inn's North

HAY RIVER, Northwest Territories
- Ptarmigan Inn
- H.R. Dene Band Reserve, Sharing Lodge

OLD CROW, Yukon
- Yukon College

LABRADOR / NORTHERN QUEBEC

May 28, 1992

NAIN, Labrador
- Grenfell Nursing Station
- Martin Group Home
- Community Hall
- Nain Nursing Station
- Paivitsiak (Nain Day Care)

May 29, 1992

POVUNGNITUK, QUEBEC
- Invulitsivik Hospital Conference Room

May 30, 1992

POVUNGNITUK, QUEBEC
- Nain School Gymnasium

May 31, 1992

POVUNGNITUK, QUEBEC
- Invulitsivik Hospital

June 1, 1992

INUKJUAK, QUEBEC
- Mayor's Office

June 2, 1992

KUIJJUARAPIK, QUÉBEC
- Private home

B. PHASE II

1. PANEL MEETING WITH NATIONAL WOMEN'S GROUPS
Ottawa, Ontario
May 25, 1992

Following the completion of a national round of consultations, some Panel members met with national women's groups to further identify a range of solutions that would be effective in eradicating violence. The purpose of the meeting was to seek further input from national organizations in order to ensure that the expertise and analysis these groups developed over the past several decades were given full recognition.

DAWN Canada Richmond, B.C.	NAWL Ottawa, Ontario
CASAC Ottawa, Ontario Vancouver, B.C.	NOIVMWC Ottawa, Ontario
FNFCF Ottawa, Ontario	LEAF Ottawa, Ontario
NAC Toronto, Ontario	YWCA Toronto, Ontario

2. JOINT MEETING OF PANEL, ADVISORY COMMITEE AND WOMEN'S GROUPS
Ottawa, Ontario
September 19-20, 1992

A document summarizing issues to be included in the Final Report and the National Action Plan was discussed.

- Association féminine d'éducation et d'action sociale

- Cercle des fermières du Québec

- Fédération des femmes du Québec (FFQ)

- Fédération des ressources d'hébergement

- Fédération nationale des femmes canadiennes-françaises (FNFCF)

- Native Women's Association of Canada (NWAC)

- Nova Scotia Association of Women's Centre (CONNECT)

- Pauktuutit Inuit Women's Association

- Provincial Association of Transition Houses of Saskatchewan (PATHS)

- Regroupement des maisons d'hébergement

- YWCA

3. ALBERTA/NWT NETWORK OF IMMIGRANT WOMEN
Edmonton, Alberta
September 26, 1992

Panel member, Mobina Jaffer, was invited to address the group. She spoke about the Panel's work, its Final Report and the National Action Plan.

4. ROUNDTABLE ON HEALTH IN THE ABORIGINAL COMMUNITY
Ottawa, Ontario
October 5, 1992

Participants representing Aboriginal health organizations were given the opportunity to discuss the Aboriginal Foundation Document. Through small group discussions, they identified gaps, tested solutions and recommendations and accumulated further research on violence related issues.

5. NATIVE WOMEN'S ASSOCIATION OF CANADA ANNUAL MEETING
Ottawa, Ontario
October 16-18, 1992

The Aboriginal Circle was given time on the agenda to present its Foundation Document for comment and input.

6. ROUNDTABLE WITH ELDERS OF THE ABORIGINAL COMMUNITY
Kahnawake, Quebec
October 20-21, 1992

The purpose of the roundtable was to develop a national network of elders to focus on issues of healing the individual, the family and the community. The Foundation Document was used to identify gaps and test solutions and recommendations.

Theresa Augustine
Big Cove,
New Brunswick

Shirley Bear
Perth-Andover,
New Brunswick

Ernie Benedict
Cornwall,
Ontario

Johnson Blacksmith
Cross Lake,
Manitoba

Winnie Cockney
Inuvik,
NWT

Elizabeth Colin
Fort McPherson,
Yukon

William Commanda
Maniwaki,
Quebec

Diane Kay*
Inuvik,
NWT

Peal Keenan
Whitehorse,
Yukon

Ernie Knockwood
Cape Breton,
Nova Scotia

Harold Laporte
Fredericton,
New Brunswick

Ed Louie
Keremeos,
British Columbia

Mary Louie
Keremeos,
British Columbia

Liza Mosher
Sudbury,
Ontario

Lena Nottaway
Rapid Lake,
Quebec

Peter O'Chiese
Whitehorse,
Yukon

Maggie Paul
Fredericton,
New Brunswick

Alan Paupanekis*
Cross Lake,
Manitoba

Marie Ross
Ottawa,
Ontario

Herman Saulis
Fredericton,
New Brunswick

Geraldine Stand-up
Kahnawake,
Quebec

Flora Tabagon
Parry Sound,
Ontario

Leslie Tabagon*
Toronto,
Ontario

Gordon Wasteste
Regina,
Saskatchewan

Vicki Wilson
Prince Albert,
Sask.

* Attendant

7. WOMEN WITH DISABILITIES THINKTANK
Ottawa, Ontario
October 28, 1992

The purpose of the thinktank was to discuss violence issues relative to women with disabilities. A document summarizing relevant issues was reviewed. Comments were recorded and used in the development of the Final Report and the National Action Plan. Representatives of the following organizations and a number of individual experts attended.

- Canadian Association of Independent Living Centre

- CHANNAL

- CHEZ DORIS

- Council of the Disabled

- Deaf Children Society

- NWT Council for the Disabled

- Saskatchewan Voice of the Handicapped

**8. Métis Women Conference
Edmonton, Alberta**
November 27-29, 1992

*Aboriginal Circle member, Winnifred Giesbrecht,
addressed the participants of the Métis Women's
Conference. The Aboriginal Foundation
Document was presented. Feedback received was
used in the development of the Final Report and
the National Action Plan.*

9. Churches Roundtable
Ottawa, Ontario
December 1, 1992

*The Aboriginal Circle, Panel members and church
representatives met to discuss the issue of
residential schools and the role of churches in the
aboriginal community. Feedback and input was
provided for use in the development of the
National Action Plan.*

- Aboriginal Rights Coalition (ARC)

- Anglican Church of Canada

- CCCB - Catholic Bishops

- Church Council on Justice and Corrections

- Presbyterian Church of Canada

- United Church of Canada

10. Youth Roundtable
Toronto, Ontario
January 9, 1993

*A document highlighting relevant issues on young
women, date rape and education was discussed.
Feedback and input was provided for use in the
development of the National Action Plan.
Representatives from the following organizations
and independent youths participated.*

- Toronto Board of Education
  Toronto

- Canadian Teachers' Federation
  Ottawa

- Covenant House
  Toronto, Ontario

- Girl Guides of Canada
  Markham, Ontario

- YWCA
  Toronto, Ontario

11. Youth Roundtable
Ottawa, Ontario
January 15, 1993

*A document highlighting relevant issues on Young
women, date rape and education was discussed.
Feedback and input was provided for use in the
development of the National Action Plan.
Individuals and representatives from the following
organizations participated.*

- Aboriginal Youth Council of Canada
  Ottawa, Ontario

- Big Sisters Association
  Ottawa, Ontario

- Canadian Advisory Council on the Status of
  Women (CACSW)
  Edmonton, Alberta

- Canadian Advisory Council on the Status of
  Women (CACSW)
  Ottawa, Ontario

- Canadian Ethnocultural Council
  Ottawa, Ontario

- Canadian Youth Foundation
  Longueuil, Quebec

- Direction Jeunesse
  Ottawa, Ontario

- Environmental Youth Alliance
  Ottawa, Ontario

- Federation of Women's Teachers'
  Association of Ontario and Canadian
  Teachers' Federation
  Mississauga, Ontario

- Girl Guides of Canada
  Kanata, Ontario

- Girl Guides of Canada
  Nepean, Ontario

- Girl Guides of Canada
  Pointe-Claire, Québec

- Glebe Women's Issues Group
  Ottawa, Ontario

- Guides Francophones du Canada
  Montreal, Quebec

- Inuit Tapirisat of Canada
  Ottawa, Ontario

- Leaders/YWCA
  Ottawa, Ontario

- National Round Table on the Environment
  and Economy
  Ottawa, Ontario

- Organisation des femmes dans l'Association
  nationale des étudiants et étudiantes du
  Québec
  Montreal, Quebec

- Ottawa University
  Ottawa, Ontario

- Status of Women Office
  Carleton University
  Ottawa, Ontario

- St. Patrick's High School
  Ottawa, Ontario

- Student Action for Viable Earth (S.A.V.E.)
  Tour
  Ottawa, Ontario

- Women's Centre
  Carleton University
  Ottawa, Ontario

- Youth NWT
  Calgary, Alberta

- Youth representatives for the Native
  Women's Association of Canada (NWAC)
  Edmonton, Alberta

12. **PAUKTUUTIT ANNUAL GENERAL
MEETING AND INUIT TAPIRISAT OF
CANADA — HEALTH, HOUSING AND
JUSTICE ROUNDTABLE**
Happy Valley, Goosebay, Labrador
February 23-28, 1993

*Aboriginal Circle member, Martha Flaherty,
addressed the delegates and spoke of the
development of the Inuit content of the Final
Report and the Panel's goals. Through informal
consultation, the delegates provided input and
feedback on The Community Kit.*

APPENDIX B

A. SUBMISSIONS

The Panel received 105 written submissions by mail from various organizations. Included were discussion papers/reports on the causes of violence against women, descriptions or critiques of community programs, and policy recommendations for the Panel's consideration. The Panel also received correspondence from 118 individuals. For confidentiality and safety reasons, this list cannot be published.

Action Group Against Harassment and
  Discrimination in the Workplace

Alberta Council of Womens Shelters

Association des enseignantes et des enseignants
  francophones du Nouveau-Brunswick

Barrie & District Rape Crisis Line

Battered Women's Support Services

Birdsong Communications Ltd.

Bridges Employment Training Project

British Columbia Women's Institute

Canadian Advisory Council on the Status
  of Women

Canadian Association for the Advancement of
  Women and Sport and Physical Activity
  (CAAWS)

Canadian Association of Women Executives and
  Entrepreneurs

Canadian Federation of University Women,
  B.C. Council

Canadian Federation of University Women,
  Saskatoon Club

Canadian Medical Association

Canadian Nurses Association

Canadian Organisation for the Rights of
  Prostitutes (C.O.R.P.)

Chivers Greckol and Kanee
  Barristers and Solicitors,
  Department of Public Health
  City of Toronto

City Police, City of London

Coalition Against Sexual Abuse of Children

Committee Against Pornography

Hollow Water First Nations Community
  Holistic Healing Circle

Concerned Nurses for Patients Rights - Informed
  Consent - Ethics (P.R.I.C.E.)

Corporation of the City of North Vancouver

Corrections Research and Policy Development
  Branch, Ministry of the Solicitor General of
  Canada

Crabtree Corner YWCA

Crime Prevention Society, Nova Scotia
  Department of Solicitor General

Davidson Enterprises Inc.

Department of Psychiatry
  St. Boniface Hospital

Dundurn Community Legal Services

Family Service Association of Metropolitan
  Toronto

Family Services of Greater Vancouver,

Family Support Co-ordinator, Simcoe County
  Regional Council of the Ontario Association
  for Community Living

Burnt Church Family Violence Project

Family Violence Subcommittee, North York
    Inter-Agency and Community Council

Fédération des femmes du Québec

Federation of Medical Women of Canada

Federation of Women Teachers' Association of
    Ontario

Golden Women's Resource Centre

Grande Cache Transition House Society

Grey Bruce Family Violence Prevention
    Committee

Group Against Pornography (GAP), Manitoba

Hey - way' - noqu', Healing Circle for Addictions
    Society

Immigrant and Visible Minority Women Against
    Abuse

Ingamo Family Homes Inc.

Ingamo Pre-Employment Training Program

Jewish Family & Child Service

Joint Committee RE Sexual Abuse of Patients by
    Physicians

Justice Electronics

Le conseil du civisme de Montréal

L'Intersyndicale des femmes

London Caucus of the Men's Network for
    Change

London Coordinating Committee to End Woman
    Abuse

MA MAWI WI CHI ITATA Centre

Manitoba Advisory Council on the Status of
    Women

Manitoba Council on Aging

Manitoba Teachers' Society, McMaster House

Mediawatch - National Watch on Images of
    Women in the Media Inc.

MicMac Family & Children's Services of
    Nova Scotia

NA'AMAT Inc.

National Association of Canadians of Origins
    in India

Nechi Institute

New Brunswick Advisory Council on the Status
    of Women

North Shore Community Services

Ontario Association of Interval & Transition
    Houses

Open Living Unit, Burnaby Correction
    Centre for Women

Patricia Centre for Children and Youths

Popular Theatre Alliance of Manitoba

Prince Edward Island Advisory Council on the
    Status of Women

Project Safe Run Foundation, Property
    Underwriter, Special Lines Division

Race Relations & Multiculturalism, Toronto
    Board of Education

Regroupement des CLSC du Montréal
    Métropolitain

Research and Communications Associate
    Committee for Contact with the
    Government, Council of Christian Reformed
    Churches in Canada

Saskatchewan Justice - Pine Grove Correctional Centre

S.A.V.E.

Shelter & Outreach - YWCA, Peterborough, Victoria & Halburton

Sistering

Southwest Safe Shelter

Status of Women Council of NWT

Sûreté du Québec

Surrey Women for Action

The Association of Junior Leagues, Inc.

The Children's Aid Society, Treatment Group for Men

The Concept Group

The Council on Aging Ottawa-Carleton

University of Windsor

Urgence-Femmes

Vancouver Rape Relief & Women's Shelter

Vancouver Young Women's Christian Association

West Area Family Counselling, Social Services

Western Manitoba Coalition for Equality Rights in the Canadian Constitution

White Ribbon Foundation

Woman Source Consultants

Women's Employment Counselling Service of Winnipeg Inc.

Women's Health Office - McMaster University

Women's Issues Group of the University Women's Club of North York

Women's Policy Office, Government of Newfoundland & Labrador

Woodlawn Medical Consultants

Working Against Violence Everywhere

Yorkdale Secondary School and Adult Learning Centre

Yukon Association for Community Living

B. CONSULTATION SUBMISSIONS

Many written submissions were received in support of testimony heard by the Panel during consultation events. The following 245 submissions were received from organizations. We also received 164 submissions from individuals, however, for confidentiality and safety reasons, this list cannot be published.

BRITISH COLUMBIA/ALBERTA (TOUR 1)

British Columbia

ALBERTA FAMILY AND SOCIAL SERVICES
Taber Child Abuse Committee
Taber

ATIRA TRANSITION HOUSE
Richmond

BRITISH COLUMBIA NURSES UNION
Vancouver

CONGRESS OF BLACK WOMEN OF CANADA
Vancouver Chapter
Vancouver

CRABTREE CORNER, YWCA
Vancouver

CRANBROOK WOMEN'S CENTRE
Cranbrook

DISTRICT OF NORTH VANCOUVEr
Vancouver

FAMILY SCHOOL LIAISON
Taber

IMMIGRANT AND VISIBLE MINORITY WOMEN
OF B.C.
Kelowna

JUSTICE INSTITUTE FOR BRITISH COLUMBIA
THE UNIT AGAINST PORNOGRAPHY
Vancouver

KAMLOOPS WOMEN'S RESOURCE GROUP SOCIETY
Kamloops

KELOWNA FAMILY CENTRE
Kelowna

KELOWNA WOMEN'S RESOURCE CENTRE
Kelowna

KOOTENAY EAST YOUTH PROGRAM
Cranbrook

KTUNAXA/KINBASKET TRIBAL COUNCIL
St. Mary's Reserve

NORTH SHORE WOMEN'S CENTRE
Vancouver

NORTHERN COUNSELLING AND CONSULTING
SERVICES
Smithers

PRINCE GEORGE AND DISTRICT ELIZABETH FRY
SOCIETY
Prince George

SIMON FRASER UNIVERSITY
Vancouver

TABER DISTRICT OFFICE FAMILY AND SOCIAL
SERVICES
Taber

THOMPSON VALLEY FAMILY SERVICES
ASSOCIATION
Kamloops

UNIVERSITY OF B.C.
Campus Safety for Women
Vancouver

VI LUCAN - ALDERMAN (DISTRICT OF ELKFORD)
Cranbrook

WOMEN'S COMMITTEE, S.U.C.C.E.S.S.
Vancouver

WOMEN'S EMERGENCY SHELTER
Kamloops

Alberta

SETTLER SCHOOL DISTRICT
Camrose

SUPERINTENDENT OF SCHOOLS
Camrose

WOMEN'S EMERGENCY ACCOMMODATION
CENTRE
Edmonton

QUEBEC
(TOUR 2)

A.Q.D.R.
Jonquière

ASSISTANCE AUX FEMMES DE MONTRÉAL
Montreal

ASSOCIATION DES RESSOURCES INTERVENANT
AUPRES DES HOMMES VIOLENTS (ARIHV)
Montreal

ASSOCIATION DE MONTRÉAL POUR LA
DÉFICIENCE INTELLECTUELLE
Montreal

BUSINESS AND PROFESSIONAL WOMEN'S CLUB
OF MONTRÉAL
Montreal

C.A.V.A.C. - CENTRE D'AIDE AUX VICTIMES
D'ACTES CRIMINELS
Jonquière

CONSEIL CONSULTATIF CANADIEN SUR LE STATUT
DE LA FEMME
Quebec

CENTRE DE FEMMES LA SOURCE INC.
Roberval

CLSC DE LA JONQUIÈRE
Jonquière

ÉCOLE DE PSYCHOLOGIE, UNIVERSITÉ LAVAL
Quebec

LE REGROUPEMENT PROVINCIAL DES MAISONS
D'HEBERGEMENT ET DE TRANSITION POUR FEMMES
VICTIMES DE VIOLENCE CONJUGALE
Montreal

LES CERCLES DE FERMIÈRES DU QUÉBEC
Quebec

RÉCIF - 02
Roberval

SECOURS AUX FEMMES
Montreal

UNIVERSITÉ CONCORDIA - WOMEN'S CENTRE
Montreal

VICTIMES DE POLYTECHNIQUE
Montreal

ATLANTIC REGION
(TOUR 3)

New Brunswick

BIG COVE FIRST NATION
Big Cove

FACULTY OF LAW, UNIVERSITY OF NEW
BRUNSWICK AD HOC COMMITTEE ON GENDER
RELATED POLICY
Fredericton

FAMILY VIOLENCE TREATMENT NETWORK
Fredericton, New Brunswick

FREDERICTON RAPE CRISIS CENTRE
Fredericton

LA COALITION
Bathurst

MURIEL MCQUEEN FERGUSSON FOUNDATION
Fredericton

NEW BRUNSWICK ADVISORY COUNCIL ON THE
STATUS OF WOMEN
Moncton

NEW BRUNSWICK NURSES UNION
Fredericton

SAINT JOHN POLICE FORCE
FAMILY PROTECTION UNIT
Saint John

WOMEN IN TRANSITION HOUSE INC.
Fredericton

WOMEN WORKING WITH IMMIGRANT WOMEN
Fredericton

Nova Scotia

ACADIA UNIVERSITY
Kentville

AD SUM HOUSE
Halifax

ANTIGONISH WOMEN'S RESOURCE
Antigonish

BYRONY HOUSE
Halifax

DALHOUSIE LEGAL SERVICES
Halifax

ELIZABETH FRY SOCIETY, CAPE BRETON
Sydney

FAMILY SERVICES ASSOCIATION
Halifax

GUYSBOROUGH LEARNING OPPORTUNITIES FOR
WOMEN
New Glasgow/ Antigonish

HEATHER HENDERSON
(REGIONAL REPRESENTATIVE AND STAFF NURSE
AT THE GRACE HOSPITAL)
Halifax

HORIZON HOUSE
Kentville

INSTITUTE FOR THE STUDY OF WOMEN
MOUNT SAINT VINCENT UNIVERSITY
Halifax

KENTVILLE POLICE SERVICE
Kentville

L'ASSOCIATION DES ACADIENNES DE LA
NOUVELLE-ÉCOSSE
Halifax

NAOMI SOCIETY FOR VICTIMS OF
FAMILY VIOLENCE
Antigonish

NOVA SCOTIA ADVISORY COUNCIL ON THE
STATUS OF WOMEN
Halifax

PRESIDENT'S ADVISORY COMMITTEE ON SEXUAL
HARASSMENT
Kentville

PROJECT NEW START
Halifax

PUBLIC SERVICE ALLIANCE OF CAPE BRETON
REGIONAL WOMEN'S COMMITTEE
Sydney

SECOND STORY WOMEN'S CENTRE
Bridgewater

SINGLE PARENT CENTRE
Halifax

SOUTH SHORE SURVIVORS OF CHILD
SEXUAL ABUSE
Bridgewater

SOUTH WEST NOVA TRANSITION HOUSE
ASSOCIATION, JUNIPER HOUSE
Bridgewater

TEARMANN SOCIETY FOR BATTERED WOMEN
New Glasgow

THE FAMILY VIOLENCE COMMITTEE OF
COMMUNITY AGENCIES
New Glasgow

THE HALIFAX TRANSITION HOUSE ASSOCIATION
FOR ABUSED WOMEN AND THEIR CHILDREN
Halifax

THE RED DOOR
Kentville

TRANSITION HOUSE ASSOCIATION OF
INOVA SCOTIA
Halifax

TRANSITION HOUSE ASSOCIATION OF
NOVA SCOTIA
New Glasgow

TRINITY UNITED CHURCH
New Glasgow

WOMEN'S INSTITUTES OF NOVA SCOTIA
Truro

Newfoundland

BAY ST. GEORGE WOMEN'S COUNCIL
(COMMITTEE ON ISSUES OF VIOLENCE)
Stephenville

CENTRAL NEWFOUNDLAND REGIONAL
COMMITTEE ON FAMILY VIOLENCE
St.John's

COALITION OF CITIZENS AGAINST PORNOGRAPHY
St. John's

INTERAGENCY COMMITTEE ON VIOLENCE
AGAINST WOMEN AND PROVINCIAL ASSOCIATION
AGAINST FAMILY VIOLENCE
St.John's

IRIS KIRBY HOUSE
St. John's

RCMP
Stephenville

MENTAL HEALTH SERVICES
Gander

WOMEN'S POLICY OFFICE
St.John's

Prince Edward Island

LENNOX ISLAND MICMAC RESERVE
O'Leary

THE EDITOR
O'Leary

ONTARIO
(TOUR 4)

ANNEX WOMEN'S ACTION COMMITTEE
Toronto

APPLE HOUSE
Oshawa

ASSOCIATION FÉMININE D'ÉDUCATION ET
D'ACTION SOCIALE
Ottawa

ATENLOS FAMILY VIOLENCE CENTRE
London

B'NAI BRITH WOMEN OF CANADA
Toronto

CANADIAN ASSOCIATION FOR THE ADVANCEMENT
OF WOMEN IN SPORT AND PHYSICAL ACTIVITY
Ottawa

CANADIAN RESEARCH INSTITUTE FOR THE
ADVANCEMENT OF WOMEN
Ottawa

CANADIAN ABORTION RIGHTS ACTION LEAGUE
(CARAL)
Ottawa

CASANDRA (COALITION AGAINST SEXIST AND
RACIST ADVERTISING)
Toronto

CATHOLIC FAMILY SERVICES
Downsview

DENISE HOUSE
Oshawa

DEPARTMENT OF SOCIAL SERVICES
REGION OF DURHAM
Toronto

DEVELOPMENT INITIATIVES INC.
Guelph

DUNDURN COMMUNITY LEGAL SERVICES
Hamilton

ELGIN COUNTY DELEGATION FORUM
London

FAMILY TRANSITION PLACE
Orangeville

FAMILY SERVICES CENTRE
Ottawa

FAMILY VIOLENCE MANAGEMENT SERVICE
OF CATULPA TAMARAC CHILD & FAMILY
SERVICE AGENCY
Simcoe County

FÉDÉRATION DES FEMMES CANADIENNES -
FRANÇAISES
Ottawa

FRESH START MEN'S GOUP - HIATUS HOUSE
Windsor\Chatham, Ontario

GLOUCESTER POLICE SERVICE
Ottawa

HELEN KELLY COMMUNITY HEALTH UNIT
Orangeville

HIGH SCHOOL STUDENTS
THE ONTARIO SECONDARY SCHOOL STUDENTS'
ASSOCIATION'S PROJECT B.A.S.E.
Orangeville

IMMIGRANT WOMEN AND REFUGEE WOMEN
Toronto

IMMIGRANT WOMEN AND WOMEN OF COLOR
Toronto

LABOUR COUNCIL OF METROPOLITAN TORONTO
& YORK REGION
Toronto

L'ACCUEIL FRANCOPHONE DE THUNDER BAY
Thunder Bay

MATCH INTERNATIONAL CENTRE
Ottawa

METRAC (METRO ACTION COMMITTEE ON
PUBLIC VIOLENCE AGAINST WOMEN
AND CHILDREN)
Toronto

MOTHERS ON TRIAL
Toronto

MY SISTER'S PLACE TRANSITION HOUSE
Alliston

MY FRIEND'S HOUSE
Collingwood

NATIONAL COUNCIL OF WOMEN
Ottawa

NATIVE WOMEN'S ASSOCIATION OF CANADA
Ottawa

NORTH YORK WOMEN'S CENTRE
Toronto

OJIBWAY FAMILY RESOURCE CENTRE
North Bay

OTTAWA RAPE CRISIS CENTRE
Ottawa

OTTAWA REGIONAL WOMEN'S COMMITTEE
PUBLIC SERVICE ALLIANCE OF CANADA
Ottawa

OTTAWA MULTICULTURAL HOMEMAKERS
ASSOCIATION
Ottawa

PAUKTUUTIT (INUIT WOMEN'S ASSOCIATION
OF CANADA)
Ottawa

PERTH COUNTY SHELTER
Perth

RESOURCES AGAINST PORNOGRAPHY
Toronto

RIVERDALE IMMIGRANT WOMEN'S CENTRE
   Toronto

SCARBOROUGH CULTURAL INTERPRETER SERVICE
   Scarborough

SEXUAL ABUSE SURVIVORS OF HALDIMAND-
NORFOLK
   Perth

Sexual Assault Centre of Guelph-Wellington
Women In Crisis
   Guelph

SEXUAL ASSAULT CRISIS CENTRE
   Windsor

SOUTH ASIA FAMILY SUPPORT SERVICES
   Scarborough

SUBCOMMITTEE ON THE NEEDS OF ADULT
SURVIVORS OF CHILD SEXUAL ABUSE
   Guelph

SWAN (STOP WOMAN ABUSE NOW)
   Goderich

THE CANADIAN HOME ECONOMICS ASSOCIATION
   Ottawa

"THE CHURCH LEADERS'" CONFERENCE OF
CATHOLIC BISHOPS
   Ottawa

THE DECEMBER 6TH COALITION REGION
OF WATERLOO
   Toronto

THE GUELPH CHAPTER OF THE CANADIAN
FEDERATION OF UNIVERSITY WOMEN
   Guelph

THE HEALING CENTRE FOR WOMEN
   Ottawa

THE KINGSTON PORNOGRAPHY ACTION
COMMITTEE
   Kingston

THE ONTARIO NATIVE WOMEN'S ASSOCIATION
   Thunder Bay

THE SEXUAL ASSAULT SUPPORT CENTRE
   Ottawa

THE WOMEN'S PROJECT
THE AIDS COMMITTEE OF OTTAWA
   Ottawa

TORONTO SAFE CITY COMMITTEE
   Toronto

TORONTO WOMEN IN FILM & TELEVISION
   Toronto

VICTIMS ADVOCATE
   Ottawa

VICTIM\WITNESS ASSISTANCE PROGRAM
   Windsor

VICTIM WITNESS ASSISTANCE PROGRAM, CROWN
ATTORNEY'S OFFICE, VICTIM SERVICES, WINDSOR
POLICE SERVICES

SEXUAL ASSAULT TREATMENT CENTRE,
GRACE HOSPITAL
SEXUAL ASSAULT CRISIS CENTRE
   Windsor

VIVA ASSOCIATES
   Toronto

WARKWORTH INSTITUTION - THE LIVING GROUP
   Campbellford

W.A.V.E.
   Toronto

WINDSOR WOMEN'S INCENTIVE CENTRE
   Windsor\Chatham

WOMEN'S EMERGENCY CENTRE
   Woodstock

WORK & FAMILY LIFE COMMITTEE ADVISORY
COMMITTEE FOR EQUITY
   Toronto

YWCA
   Hamilton

YWCA OF TORONTO
   Toronto

ZONTA CENTRE
Ottawa

SASKATCHEWAN/MANITOBA
(TOUR 5)

Saskatchewan

ANGLICAN PARISH OF INDIAN HEAD
Fort Qu'Appelle

CHILDREN'S HAVEN, CHILD CRISIS CENTRE
Prince Albert

CONGRESS OF BLACK WOMEN (REGINA CHAPTER)
Regina

DISABLED WOMEN'S NETWORK (DAWN)
Regina

FACULTY OF SOCIAL WORK
UNIVERSITY OF REGINA
Regina

FRESH START SEX OFFENDER PROGRAM
Saskatoon

IMMIGRANT WOMEN OF SASKATCHEWAN
Prince Albert

IMMIGRANT WOMEN OF SASKATCHEWAN
Saskatoon

INDIAN HEALTH CENTRE INC.
North Battleford

LA RONGE NATIVE WOMEN'S COUNCIL
La Ronge

LLOYDMINSTER COMMITTEE FOR THE TREATMENT
AND PREVENTION OF FAMILY VIOLENCE NEEDS
ASSESSMENT
North Battleford

LLOYDMINSTER INTERVAL HOME SOCIETY
North Battleford

LUTHER COLLEGE
Moose Jaw/Swift Current

MAYOR'S TASK FORCE ON FAMILY VIOLENCE
Prince Albert

MEADOW LAKE TRIBAL COUNCIL, MEADOW
LAKE DISTRICT TREATY INDIAN WOMEN'S GROUP
Meadow Lake

NORTH EAST CRISIS INTERVENTION CENTRE
Melfort

NORTHERN MEDICAL SERVICES
Meadow Lake

NORTHERN WOMEN'S RESOURCE SERVICE INC.
Prince Albert

ROMAN CATHOLIC ARCHDIOCESE OF REGINA
SOCIAL JUSTICE DEPT.
Regina

SASKATCHEWAN HUMAN RIGHTS COMMISSION
Saskatoon

SASKATCHEWAN WOMEN'S INSTITUTES
Saskatoon

SASKATCHEWAN VOICE OF THE HANDICAPPED
Saskatoon

SASKATOON COUNCIL OF WOMEN
Saskatoon

SASKATOON SEXUAL ASSAULT AND
INFORMATION CENTRE
Saskatoon

SEXUAL ASSAULT SERVICES OF SASKATCHEWAN
Saskatoon

SOPHIA HOUSE
Regina

SWIFT CURRENT SHELTER
Moose Jaw\Swift Current

THE EMERGENCY SHELTER FOR WOMEN
Prince Albert

THE SOUTHWEST SAFE SHELTER
Moose Jaw\Swift Current

YWCA OF SASKATOON
Saskatoon

Manitoba

AGE AND OPPORTUNITY (E.A.R.C.)
Winnipeg

CANADIAN MENTAL HEALTH ASSOCIATION -
WOMEN AND MENTAL HEALTH WORK GROUP
Winnipeg

BRANDON SHELTER
Brandon

BRANDON TEACHERS' ASSOCIATION - EQUALITY
IN EDUCATION COMMITTEE
Brandon

BRANDON UNIVERSITY STUDENT'S UNION
Brandon

BRANDON MENTAL HEALTH SERVICE
Brandon

CONGRESS OF BLACK WOMEN OF MANITOBA
Winnipeg

CROSS LAKE BAND OF INDIANS
Cross Lake

CROSS LAKE EDUCATION AUTHORITY
Cross Lake

CHURCHILL HEALTH CENTRE
Churchill

FAMILY VIOLENCE - LAKESHORE WIFE ABUSE
COMMITTEE
Lundar

FEDERATION OF JUNIOR LEAGUES OF CANADA
Winnipeg

GAP (GROUP AGAINST PORNOGRAPHY)
Winnipeg

INDIGENOUS WOMEN'S COLLECTIVE
Winnipeg

KEEWATIN TRIBAL COUNCIL
Thompson

MANITOBA ACTION COMMITTEE ON THE STATUS
OF WOMEN
Brandon

MANITOBA ACTION COMMITTEE ON THE STATUS
OF WOMEN
Winnipeg

MANITOBA ADVISORY COUNCIL ON THE STATUS
OF WOMEN
Winnipeg

MANITOBA ASSOCIATION OF WOMEN
AND THE LAW
Winnipeg

MANITOBA INTERFAITH IMMIGRATION COUNCIL
Winnipeg

MANITOBA TEACHER'S SOCIETY
Winnipeg

MIAMI COLLEGIATE
Morden

NATIVE WOMEN'S TRANSITION CENTRE
Winnipeg

NONGAM/IKWE
Winnipeg

NORTHERN WOMEN'S RESOURCE SERVICE INC
The Pas

PARKLAND CRISIS CENTRE
Dauphin

PARKLAND STATUS OF WOMEN
Dauphin

POWER - PROSTITUTES AND OTHER WOMEN FOR
EQUAL RIGHTS
Winnipeg

RÉSEAU
Winnipeg

SOUTHWEST CRISIS SERVICES INC.
Winnipeg

THOMPSON CRISIS CENTRE
    Garden Hill

YOUNG WOMEN'S CHRISTIAN ASSOCIATION
(YWCA) OF BRANDON
    Brandon

NORTHWEST TERRITORIES
(TOUR 6)

Northwest Territories

ANNETTE DOWLING & ASSOCIATES
SOCIAL WORK CONSULTANTS
    Fort Smith

ARVIAT FAMILY VIOLENCE COMMITTEE
    Rankin Inlet

CANADIAN MENTAL HEALTH ASSOCIATION/
NWT DIVISION
    Yellowknife

KATAUJAQ SOCIETY
    Rankin Inlet

NORTHERN ADDICTION SERVICES -
TREATMENT CENTRE
    Yellowknife

ROMAN CATHOLIC DIOCESE OF MACKENZIE
    Yellowknife

STATUS OF WOMEN COUNCIL OF THE NWT
    Yellowknife

Yukon

CANADIAN RESEARCH INSTITUTE FOR THE
ADVANCEMENT OF WOMEN
    Whitehorse

EARLY CHILDHOOD DEVELOPMENT PROGRAM
YUKON COLLEGE
    Whitehorse

KAUSHEE'S WOMEN'S SHELTER PLACE
    Whitehorse

LESBIAN ISSUE COMMITTEE
    Whitehorse

MINISTER RESPONSIBLE FOR THE STATUS
OF WOMEN, YUKON MINISTER OF JUSTICE
    Whitehorse

VIOLENCE AGAINST WOMEN COLLECTIVE OF
YUKON STATUS OF WOMEN'S COUNCIL
    Whitehorse

WOLVERINE CONSULTING CO. LTD.
    Whitehorse

YUKON ADVISORY COUNCIL ON WOMEN'S ISSUES
    Whitehorse

YUKON COLLEGE, TESLIN CAMPUS
    Teslin

APPENDIX C

PANEL DOCUMENTS AND PRODUCTS*

Ending Violence Against Women...
Your Chance To Do Something About It !
Consultations by the Canadian Panel on Violence
Against Women

A Progress Report

The Road to Healing (Map)
(Cree, Oji-Cree, Inuktituk, English and French)

A Landscape of Violence (Map)

Collecting the Voices: A Scrapbook

Changing the Landscape: Ending Violence —
Achieving Equality
Final Report of the Canadian Panel on Violence
Against Women

Changing the Landscape: Ending Violence —
Achieving Equality
Executive Summary\National Action Plan

Changing the Landscape — Inuit Chapter
(Inuktituk - Syllabic and Orthography, English)

Changing the Landscape — Aboriginal Chapter
(Cree, English and French)

Without Fear
(video)

Without Fear - Video Facilitator's Guide

The Community Kit

RESEARCH PAPERS CONTRACTED BY THE CANADIAN PANEL ON VIOLENCE AGAINST WOMEN

Adult Survivors of Child Sexual Abuse/Incest
Linda McLeod and Associates

Aspects of Canadian Popular Culture:
Messages About Violence and Gender
Behaviour
Sandra Campbell

Elder Abuse
Linda McLeod and Asssociates

Inuit Women: The Realities and Issues
Surrounding Violence Against Women
Sophie Tom

Pornography
Jillian Ridington

Ritual Abuse
Daniela Coates

Sexual Assault
Linda McLeod and Associates

Violence Against Foreign Domestic Workers in
Canada
Judith Nicholson

Violence Against Immigrant Women of Colour
Fauzia Rafiq

Violence Against Lesbians: Issues and Solutions
Adonica Huggins

Violence Against Native Women
Teressa Nahanee

Violence Against Women and Sexual
Harassment
Anne Robinson and Monique Gauvin

Violence Against Women in Rural Settings
Wendy Milne

Violence Against Women of Colour
Rozena Maart

All materials produced in English and French unless otherwise indicated.

Wife Assault
Linda McLeod and Associates

**Women's Safety Project : A Community-Based
Study of Sexual Violence in Women's Lives -
Summary of Key Statistical Findings**
Melanie Randall and Lori Haskell

**Young Women and Violence:
A Collective Response**
Francine Lavoie

**Report on Findings From the Householder
Survey produced by:**
The Coopers & Lybrand Consulting Group in
conjunction with The Canadian Panel on
Violence Against Women

Date Due